Cry God for Larry

As a personal friend and as the Press Representative of the National Theatre, Virginia Fairweather has known Sir Laurence Olivier for more than twenty years. She is thus the ideal person to provide us with an intimate memoir of our greatest contemporary actor, both in his professional and private life.

Writing in a scintillating and revealing style, itself reminiscent of the energy and excitement of the theatre world, Mrs. Fairweather portrays Olivier as a man of wisdom and sensitivity—witty, kind, considerate or stern, as the occasion demanded. Her fascinating story takes us through the difficult days of his post-war professional career; his turbulent divorce from Vivien Leigh and his happy marriage to Joan Plowright; the creation of the Chichester Festival Theatre and the inception of the National; the difficulties of the National's first triumphal overseas tour with its shattering internal wrangles, and the illness which Sir Laurence has so courageously overcome.

While essentially a personal memoir, Cry God for Larry records Sir Laurence's participation in some of the most decisive developments in the English theatre over the last two decades, and thereby provides an important contribution to the theatrical chronicles of this exciting period. The addition of many hitherto unpublished photographs illuminates the text in an interesting and informative way.

VIRGINIA FAIRWEATHER

Cry God
for
Larry

An intimate memoir of Sir Laurence Olivier

CALDER & BOYARS · LONDON

First published in Great Britain in 1969 by
Calder and Boyars Ltd
18 Brewer Street London W1

© 1969, Virginia Fairweather

SBN 7145 0000 3 Cloth bound edition

Printed in Great Britain by
Western Printing Services Ltd, Bristol

PICTURE CREDITS:

Berliner Ensemble; Chichester Photographic Service; Stan Goozee;
Charles Howard; Keystone Press; Angus McBean; Daily Mail;
Portsmouth Evening News; David Sim; Southern Publishing Co;
Hans Wild; Wool Secretariat.

To L.

with my love for always

CONTENTS

LIST OF ILLUSTRATIONS

9

5b '*I cannot tell what the dickens his name is*'

Part of the line-up to meet the Queen after Uncle Vanya. *Olivier as Astrov, introduces Ivan Alderman, Diana Boddington, David Fairweather, the Author and Laurier Lister.*

6a '*And so, my good Lord Mayor, a pleasant time of day*'

Olivier chatting to the Mayor of Chichester, Councillor J. M. Selby, after the Cathedral Commemoration Service. In the background are Mr. and Mrs. Jim Battersby, the Earl of Bessborough (Chairman) and Joan Plowright.

6b '*Good Nurse, thou art a paragon of women*'

Sybil Thorndike and Laurence Olivier in Uncle Vanya. *One of Larry's favourite pictures.*

7a '*Well said: that was laid on with a* trowel'

The Mills family—John, Hayley and Mary—being interviewed on the opening night of Chichester.

7b '*Had you an eye behind you, you might see detraction at your heels*'

John Dexter directing Joan Plowright and Jeremy Brett in Saint Joan.

8 '*Fat paunches have lean pates*'

Olivier in Semi-Detached *struggling to keep up with the Birmingham Joneses.*

Following page 128

9a '*Nay, good uncle of Norfolk, what's o'clock?*'

The Queen, Prince Philip and the Duke and Duchess of Norfolk arriving early for the gala performance of Uncle Vanya.

9b *'So in our Windsor Castle make we merry'*

Olivier with A. T. Smith (Chairman of the London Committee) and the Author raising funds aboard the Windsor Castle *at Southampton.*

10a *'To business that we love, we rise betime and go to't with delight'*

The Duke of Norfolk and Olivier with Princess Margaret and Lord Snowdon who had arrived by helicopter to attend a charity performance of Saint Joan.

10b *'And 'tis not hard, I think,*
For men so old as we to keep the peace'

Kenneth Tynan (Literary Manager), Lord Chandos (Chairman), Olivier (Director) and Stephen Arlen (Administrator) at the first press conference in the 'huts' of the National Theatre, 1963.

11 *'God hath given you one face, and you make yourself another'*
The most publicised picture of Olivier in Othello.

12a *'I do perceive here a divided duty!'*
Lord Chandos as the host with the Author greeting Helene Weigel at a party for the Berliner Ensemble at the Old Vic rehearsal room.

12b *'How does your honour for this many a day?*
The last night of the Berliner season and Olivier meets Helene Weigel in the dressing-room.

Following page 160

13a *'Why, that's my spirit!'*
Olivier, in borrowed uniform, marshalling his Company on board en route for Moscow.

13b *'Speak not—lest foreign ears attend thee!'*
The Ukraine Hotel, Moscow. The top seven floors are devoted to 'bugging'.

14 *'This will last out the night in Russia!'*

Olivier and Billie Whitelaw on-stage at the opening of Othello, *still acknowledging the audience after thirty-five minutes' applause.*

15a *'I have a reasonable good ear in music'*

Larry relaxing with the Ambassador, Sir Geoffrey Harrison, in the British Embassy after the first night.

15b *'What news on the Rialto?'*

A section of G.U.M., the vast arcade store which is stuffed with nothing worth buying.

16a *'He draweth out the thread of his verbosity!'*

Nicolas Nabokov, Artistic Director of the Berliner Festwochen, speaking at a press conference at the Kempinski Hotel, West Berlin.

16b *'I have done the state some service, but no more of that.*

Farewell! Virginia's occupation's gone!'

Cry God for Larry

I

Opening Scenes

DURING the war I took part in one of those All-Star Charity Concerts at the London Palladium. The item from the intimate revue in which I was appearing with the two Hermiones —Baddeley and Gingold—was the 'grand finale' to the matinée. When it finished I rushed to my dressing-room and started to remove my make-up. There was a tap on the door and my dresser told me that an extremely handsome officer wished to see me, adding in a warning whisper, that he had a young lady with him. I asked her to show him in; that was the first time Laurence Olivier and I met. Of course the 'young lady' was his wife, Vivien Leigh. He introduced himself and stayed for some while. When they left I was overwhelmed with pleasure and amazement that he had taken the trouble to come round and encourage an unknown actress. In later years I discovered that this unconscious flattery is part of his enormous magnetism, which makes those who come in contact with him feel a little happier and a little more important within themselves. After the war had ended a great friend of mine, David Fairweather—later to become my husband—invited me to the first night of *The School for Scandal* at the New Theatre, as he was the press representative for the production. This was a thrilling invitation because it was impossible to obtain tickets for it; the

15

galleryites had queued overnight, an unheard-of thing in those days. At the end of the performance, David asked me if I would like to accompany him backstage. One of the star dressing-rooms was packed with the usual first night crowd, we managed to push our way through, and David said 'Larry, I would like you to meet Virginia.'

Although I couldn't know it then this second meeting with the recently knighted Sir Laurence Olivier marked an association which was to continue for the next twenty years. While the season lasted it became a frequent habit to drop into their dressing-rooms. In those days I found Vivien much easier to get on with than Larry. She was an extrovert; intelligent, gay and amusing, with a biting tongue. I had no inkling that I would ever become a publicist myself but enough knowledge to realise that an actor's co-operation with the press was of vital importance. Perhaps her understanding of that endeared her to me in the first place. When Larry decided he wouldn't be photographed she would circumvent his edict and smooth the situation by saying to David 'Never mind, Feathers, ask them if they would like pictures of me. It's such fun to hear those flash-bulbs—pop, pop, pop, like champagne—knowing you'll never see the horrid results!'

When Larry made his spectacular success as Richard III that year, Vivien appeared in the relatively small part of the Lady Anne. She was passionately addicted to the current card game of canasta. This was played with a limited circle of chums during the performances of *Richard*. Although concentrating hard, she tended to become highly voluble. One matinée Larry came into her room looking jolly fearsome as Richard and remonstrated with her to make less noise as their dressing-rooms were on stage level. Hot in the lead, and winning hands down, she smiled up at him very sweetly and in dulcet tones said 'My darling, you wouldn't hear if you closed the door.' He roared with laughter and left—carefully closing the door behind him. During this season Larry and Vivien were planning to rent a theatre of their own and present plays themselves. Eventually they secured a lease on the St. James's; a beautiful old playhouse with a great tradition, great elegance and great pillars that obscured one's view. The opening production was a verse play by Christopher Fry entitled *Venus Observed*. This had been commissioned some time earlier and had originally been intended to incorporate parts for both of them. The play took longer to finish than had been anticipated. Meanwhile Vivien had opened in *A Streetcar Named Desire*, which was still running very successfully, therefore Larry had to rethink ideas for his leading lady. He chose a relatively unknown actress called Heather Stannard whose looks resembled Vivien's in a vague way. During rehearsals, quite unaware that she was a substitute for Vivien, she developed complexes about her face and her voice. Although very attractive she was not a 'great beauty'. She was sent to Angus McBean, the most brilliant portrait photographer, to have some pictures taken; Larry tore up all the proofs from the first sitting and sent her back. Finally, from dozens of shots, he passed two. This and his insistence on 'how-now-brown-cow' exercises robbed her of much self-confidence. In present times these quibbles would not apply since it is fashionable to make oneself look odd and almost essential to have a flat regional accent. Although the war was over there was still certain rationing and austerity, but the Oliviers decided to make the St. James's Theatre, while under their management, a notable exception to the accustomed drabness, regardless of expense. Money was lavished both on the production and the floral-banked interior of the theatre. Vivien made it clear that she would like their entourage to wear white tie and tails for the opening

17

night. Two of them did and looked fairly silly. Perhaps shades of the great actor-managers of the past echoed in the Oliviers' minds.

We were invited to spend a weekend at Notley Abbey, their country house near Thame. It was relaxed and informal with much witty conversation, liberally sprinkled with colourful epithets. Late on Sunday night Vivien delivered a lecture on the paucity of our vocabulary and our excessive use of swear words. We solemnly agreed with her and promised to remedy our speech in future. Next morning, on the way to town, Larry suddenly shouted 'Fork right!' then leaned back and hastily apologised for his lapse.

The Oliviers had contracted to go to Hollywood to make films—and some much needed dough to help subsidise the St. James's Theatre. They planned to return to England in the spring to present one or possibly two productions during the Festival of Britain. Mad ideas had been bandied about but none so apparently mad as the final decision: to produce Shaw's *Cleopatra* followed by Shakespeare's the subsequent evening. Larry took David to supper one night to discuss some of the problems involved. They were attended by an over-impressive and fussy little waiter who hovered like an anxious moth as they tried to talk, shifting a horrid red table-lamp from side to side. Finally Larry hissed 'What the hell does he think I'm going to do? Sink my teeth into your lovely white shoulder?' Shattered, the man withdrew. Among the illustrious cast assembled for the two plays was the divine, eccentric actor Wilfrid Hyde White. He was to be Britannus in *Caesar and Cleopatra* and, loth and reluctant, had been persuaded to undertake the small role of Lemprius Euphonius in *Antony and Cleopatra*. He informed us that he couldn't remember that mouthful of a name; didn't know what the play was about; and couldn't come in on cue because he didn't understand what people were saying to him. We asked how he got on with the two stars. Almost accusingly he replied, 'You said I'd like him. I like HER but I can't get on with HIM—the little feller never seems to talk.' Before the two first nights Larry issued stern warnings to the company that they were not to go to any party after Caesar, all celebrations were to be reserved for the end of Antony. This advice was certainly followed by Larry and Vivien themselves but, after the plays had been launched, Vivien threw herself into an orgy of entertaining. She was a born hostess and adored having people round her. Sometimes this got too much for Larry who, tired after a performance, would have dearly loved to go quietly home instead of putting on his dinner jacket and having to be social.

At the conclusion of the London season of the *Cleopatras* they took the plays to New York, having arranged to present Orson Welles in *Othello* at the St. James's. This seemed a wonderful idea and we anticipated it with eagerness. At the end of the first reading, as Mr. Welles prepared to tuck in to a light five-course lunch sent from The Ivy, David asked for two minutes' chat, explaining who he was. To his surprise he was told brusquely to communicate with him through one of his secretaries. Not exactly helpful, but Peter Finch and Maxine Audley were also in the cast and more co-operative. Following a stormy, hotel-shaken tour it opened at the St. James's in the middle of October. The theatre was packed with an expectant audience to see Orson Welles's first appearance on the English stage. A few minutes after the curtain had gone up a herculean figure enveloped in a dusty black velvet garment was seen at the top of a flight of stairs. He advanced a few steps, peered over the balustrade with puzzlement on his face and, in a loud voice, said 'Fuck!' and retreated. He had made his London début, but a little early.

19

There was an audible gasp from the first few rows of stalls and a lot of whispering; of *course* it had been imagined. The one who knew it hadn't was Peter Finch and he was too nervous to do more than glance a trifle apprehensively towards the rostrum and hope for the best. At rehearsals Orson, who had also directed the play, had purposely left the knowledge of his own movements a little vague, but I don't think he'd intended adding to the script. He played the Moor for realism: one evening, in the last act, in which he kills Desdemona, he banged Gudrun Ure's head so hard on the wooden bed that she lay in a semi-conscious daze; another night he flung prop metal coins across Maxine Audley's face, cutting it open. I don't know who was the more concerned after the curtain calls, the stage-hands by Maxine's rhetoric or Orson by what he had done.

In the New Year the Oliviers returned to England for a short rest from active work, which irked Vivien who lived to enjoy life, burning up her apparently tireless energy. The respite gave her time for social activities widely ranging from square dancing, to hiring a Thames launch to Greenwich, to appearing with Larry and John Mills in a song-and-dance act at a midnight matinée. This last exploit, unwittingly, was to have a lasting effect. For a while I had had several press enquiries asking if she was going to have a baby. I answered them in true ignorance with a firm denial. Edward Goring, a journalist then working on the *Mail*, had heard this rumour and telephoned the Oliviers' home late one night. Larry answered it in, as he put it, a heavily disguised voice. Ted Goring, sure in his own mind that he was talking to the Knight though unable to prove it, said he had heard that Vivien was going to have a baby. The reply he got was 'Reely? Oh, that will be *most* gratifying for all of us below stairs!' This finished Ted—and the conversation. Unfortunately, some while later, Vivien had a miscarriage. When she had regained her strength she agreed to make another film with locations in Ceylon and studio work in America. After some weeks we had a telephone call from Larry's manager to say that she had been taken ill and was suffering from nervous exhaustion. Larry himself and Cecil Tennant, their manager and close personal friend, had flown out to fetch her home and they were desirous, for her sake, that there should be no publicity. We were told she would be given sufficient sedatives to render her unconscious during the flight as, due to an earlier experience of a forced landing she was afraid of flying and they didn't wish to cause her further anxiety. Airport officials had been alerted and arrangements made to transport her privately from the plane to a nursing home on a stretcher. One should have known Vivien's indomitable spirit by now. There are always a number of press photographers attached to Heathrow Airport waiting for celebrities to arrive and, a short while before touching down, Vivien awoke, became aware of the situation and started making up her face in preparation for landing. To everyone's amazement, with her customary poise she walked alone down the gang-plank clutching an armful of roses and stood smiling while her picture was taken.

During her convalescence they both consented to appear in a new comedy, *The Sleeping Prince* by Terence Rattigan. Following a short provincial tour it opened in London in the autumn. Terry gave a large party in his flat after the first night. The play had been received with enthusiasm by the audience, and in the early hours of the morning Larry asked us to take his chauffeur to Fleet Street and buy the first editions with the notices. This is always a rash thing to do because public and critical reactions are not necessarily the same. One of Larry's entourage had had the same idea and taken the chauffeur, but a guest volunteered to drive us. The press, with one exception, damned the play with leavened faint praise; it was considered too flimsy in plot, and a trifle *vieux jeu* because it had one. Larry, in turn, came in for gentle criticism for choosing to appear in it: but a really savage notice was headed 'Wake Up Sleeping Prince' and seemed a personal attack without any objective judgment. We read it in the car with mounting rage, tore it up and raced back to the flat. There we found an atmosphere of Chekhovian gloom in place of the effervescent gaiety we had so recently left. The well-meaning clot had gone as far as Lyons' Corner House, bought a few papers, including the one with the bad notice, which he had circulated. Larry was the first to utter: he carefully removed his glasses and addressed Terry. 'On behalf of my wife and myself, as actors, and personally as your director, I would like to apologise, dear Terry, for mucking up your play.' Whipping off his glasses Terry replied, 'Darlings, both, on my behalf, as an author, please accept my apologies for having written such a mucky, trivial little play.' With a loud scraping back of chair bespectacled Noël Coward said, 'Children, may I say—on *all* your behalves—that as an author, producer and actor I have frequently managed to muck up my own acting, plays and productions and still survive.' There was a fractional pause before all of us burst into spontaneous laughter. Terry opened another bottle of champagne and the black mood was dispelled. Who else, I wondered, possessed that humour and understanding of the moment except Noël Coward. Bless him!

The next indirect contact I had with Larry was many months later when he was somewhere in Scotland looking for suitable locations for his proposed film of *Macbeth*. I was suddenly awakened by the telephone ringing at half past three in the morning. Sleepily I lifted it to be greeted by an accusing Scot's voice saying: 'This is the Scottish Daily Aixpress. We've lost Laurence Olivier. Can you tell us whair to faind him?' Suppressing the obvious answer, I suggested he should buy a map, hire a ghillie and three bloodhounds and stop asking me damn fool questions. Maybe not good public relations but the best I could muster at that ungodly hour.

After a season at Stratford Larry and Vivien returned to London. A few hundred yards away from the flat in Eaton Square their great friend George Devine was making theatre history at the Royal Court. In 1956 a new play, *Look Back in Anger*, by an unknown playwright, John Osborne, had opened to controversial press. In fact it provoked literal fisticuffs in the local pub involving a keen, brilliant, young critic, Kenneth Tynan. Larry saw the play and didn't like it but was persuaded by George to see it again. The second visit changed his opinion radically. He had meetings with John Osborne and asked him to write a play for him with a broken-down music-hall background as the central theme. This was finished some months later and entitled *The Entertainer*. It marked a completely new phase in Larry's career: up to this time he had been thought of primarily as a Shakespearean and classical actor rather than a 'new wave' experimentalist. The critics were unanimous about *The Entertainer*, praising both John and Larry. It was scheduled for only a limited season at the Royal Court because the Oliviers had previously contracted to tour Europe with *Titus Andronicus*, then take it to the Stoll Theatre. However, Larry agreed to a West End transfer of *The Entertainer* after *Titus*. His leading lady, Dorothy Tutin, who had originally played his daughter, was not available and the part had to be re-cast. An almost ob-

23

vious choice was Joan Plowright, one of the up-and-coming members of the Royal Court youngsters. At the first rehearsal a press photographer asked for a picture of 'Sir Laurence with his new leading lady'. Larry turned to the man and said 'She's my daughter in the play—how would you like us to pose?' 'Oh just get together' was the answer. Larry, playing the fool and wishing to be shot of the whole thing quickly, seized Joan Plowright round the waist, gripped her thigh in a lascivious fashion and held the ridiculous pose for a second.

It opened at the New Theatre and concurrently L.O.P.— Larry and Vivien's production company—had presented a play by an Australian, Ray Lawler, *The Summer of the Seventeenth Doll*, with an all Australian cast, and a comedy by Lesley Storm, *Roar Like a Dove*. To celebrate the success of the three ventures Larry and Vivien gave a party for the casts at the New. Among the famous names was the virtually unknown young actress, Joan Plowright. Although she had toured for a few weeks with the great Sir Laurence she had never met his wife. She did that night—in a perfunctory fashion. She said 'Hallo' to her.

The Entertainer ran for six months, first in London and then in New York. The following year Robert Morley was presenting a French comedy, *Hook, Line and Sinker*, and approached Joan to play his young wife. This was her first play for a strictly commercial management—if that description could ever apply to Robert. Having cast her, he said, 'The poor little thing looks pale. Sunshine would do her good. I'll take her to the South of France for a long week-end to put some colour in her cheeks—and have her hair properly done.' Not knowing Robert previously and unversed in West End procedure she, rather hesitantly, consented to this plan. She really need not have worried: they flew to Nice, Robert dropped her at a luxury hotel and, telling her he was going to have a little flutter, he ambled to the Casino. This was the last she saw of him until it was time to fly back for rehearsals the next Monday. She had had her hair restyled and looked very pretty and *very* pale.

At sporadic intervals there had been various press enquiries concerning a possible rift between the Oliviers. These, with complete conviction, I had vehemently denied. Larry had gone back to play at Stratford and Vivien was appearing in the West End. This seemed of vital interest to the press—heaven knows why because there had been many occasions when the two of them had acted apart. Possibly there had been a faint rumour, with a ring of truth, that became magnified. Quite apart from the rivalry that exists between papers to get a 'scoop' there is also the inherent human element that enjoys destroying its idols. Some months later Larry asked me if I would publicise Vivien in Noël Coward's version of a Feydeau farce, *Look After Lulu*, at the Royal Court. This was the first production I had done on my own and I was very nervous. Silly really, because Vivien was wonderful to work with. She had every sympathy with the job you were doing for her and the play, and a quick, decisive mind that could deal with problems and discard trivia. It opened in the provinces and the provincial press reported: 'She looked delicious in black fishnet tights and an Edwardian corset.' At the Royal Court it was the custom to have a general press-photograph call before the first night. I told her about this and, without any previous experience of a 'free-for-all', she agreed to pose for them for half an hour. Neither she nor I knew what we were in for: approximately fifty photographers arrayed themselves at the edge of the stage. Punctually Vivien appeared wearing a beautiful Edwardian dress. After ten minutes of fairly polite clicking the photographers started to get tough. They asked her to pull her dress down to

25

show her cleavage, which she politely declined to do; then, exasperated, they began shouting and telling her to change into the corsets and look sexy, at the same time many of them milled onto the stage. By now I was frantic and Vivien icy cold with rage. She rose from the sofa on which she had been posing and in ringing tones, addressing them as 'Gentlemen', reminded them that she had kept her word to give them facilities for taking pictures of the play but she had no intention of posing for cheesecake, and left the stage. They then turned their wrath on me and threatened to report me, have me blackballed by their editors and put a ban on any pictures of the production. I now know that was a load of hot air but it scared me at the time. I went up to Viven's dressing-room to offer my apologies at the same time as she came to the door full of apologies to *me*. We both had a calming brandy, which swiftly convinced us photographers were hell but we were lovely and that was then the end of that. But it was a lesson I never forgot.

One day Vivien showed me an article written in an Italian magazine. It was a typical scandal-sheet piece, much favoured by the foreign press, purporting to have been written by an I-was-there gentleman who, with mawkish sentimentality, expounded on the 'lonely life of the lovely Leigh left by Laurence, her lover'. She was worried that the British papers might follow it up, at the same time hastening to assure me it was untrue. Although I had been told that Larry was staying with friends, I preferred to keep up the illusion for both their sakes. In September the play transferred, strangely enough, to the New Theatre of so many memories. After the first night numerous photographers asked for a picture of Larry and Vivien together in her dressing-room. At that moment he was upstairs congratulating some other member of the cast. Asking the chaps to wait, I ran to the upper floor and seized Larry. At the best of times he was never keen to be photographed but he realised the exigency of the moment and, at once, came downstairs. I think this surprised the press; anyway a number of happy snaps were taken and they departed satisfied.

In the following spring of 1960 Vivien went to New York to star in *Duel of Angels* in which she had been enormously successful earlier in London. One Sunday evening, a few weeks later, Larry telephoned me and asked if I would be free to publicise a play he was going to do at the Royal Court called *Rhinoceros* by Eugène Ionesco. I said I would love to and he invited me round to Eaton Square for a drink. Telling David I would be away for an hour I set off. Larry was alone and asked me what I would like to drink. I replied a brandy and ginger ale. 'Fine!' he said, 'I'm drinking whisky,' and placed a bottle of cognac beside me and a bottle of Scotch on his table. Sensing something out of the ordinary was about to be discussed I tensed myself and waited. Without preamble or any feeling of constraint he told me that he had fallen deeply in love with Joan Plowright who was living apart from her husband and endeavouring to obtain a divorce. Larry was racked with worry and guilt; and horror at the unavoidable scandal that would ensue if there should be a divorce between him and Vivien. Like any man labelled 'the guilty party' he was conscience-stricken at the idea of ending a marriage that had meant so much even though it had now gone sour. Whoever was 'to blame' he didn't wish to hurt Vivien; at the same time he had terrible remorse about the harm the publicity might do to Joan. His previous marriage had been annulled when he was relatively unknown, but this time, inevitably, it would make the headlines, almost like royalty. I asked him how he would like me to deal with the press. His answer was, 'Darling, if anyone is going to come out looking like a shit let it be me. Do your best not to let them persecute Joanie or Viv.' He told me about his mother whom he had adored—she died when he was an early adolescent and had always remained a near fantasy figure; and about his attitude towards his father—concealed resentment mixed with awe and unapproachability. He talked a lot about Vivien, her belief in him and her driving ambition for him which had sustained and carried him along with her. He told me how she had broken down his innate shyness and reserve with strangers outside the theatre circle, helped him as a hostess, 'educated' him in so many ways and how grateful he would always be to her. Listening, I felt his humility, which is his strength, and sensed the regrets. Instinctively I crossed the room and kissed him. We filled our glasses and went on chatting. Quite naturally, the conversation turned to Joan: he was deeply concerned with the difference in their ages— he was fifty-two and she was thirty. I laughed and told him that was the same with David and me and it didn't count. They both wanted to have children and he couldn't envisage the future or any possible solution. Without being able to substantiate it I pledged him my own beliefs for his future and my total loyalty. I looked at my watch: I had been there four hours and I felt I had known the lifetime of a man within that space. With our last drink I said I had better return otherwise I, personally, would be divorced before I was married.

Next week I attended the first reading of *Rhinoceros*. Orson Welles was the producer and we joked and reminisced over *Othello* and I reminded him of his churlish attitude to David. 'I was a goddamned bastard to him,' he said proudly. 'But I'll just be a goddamned bitch to you!' Joan arrived with Larry and we were ceremoniously 'introduced'. We lunched together and he told her that any press enquiries should be put through to me. Many of the rehearsals were conducted at an odd church hall in Maida Vale. We had one large room with a portion curtained off, presumably a small stage, and a door leading to the church. One day we arrived back for an early run-through; prior to starting, a young fellow sauntered across the room dressed like a curate. He politely bade us all a 'Good afternoon' and vanished. While the rehearsal was in progress there was a slight pause from Larry, who had forgotten his next line, during which I heard the unmistakable click of a camera and glanced towards the black curtain. I spotted a small jagged hole with a camera lens poking through. I walked over to Orson, whispered to him and pointed to the curtain. Taking in the situation he called Larry, Joan and the stage managers over for 'notes'; then quietly told the two stage management boys to go on to the little stage, take the camera and confiscate the film. For tuppence he'd have done it himself albeit too fleshily over-indulged. Quick as a flash the boys whipped behind the curtain. There was a brief struggle and a tinkle of broken glass; then the chaps emerged struggling to hold the arms of a tough young photographer in a dark suit with his collar and tie sideways round his neck. He was swearing volubly, threatening to sue for the damaged lens, and protesting he was being obstructed from earning an honest living, adding with boastful pride he 'could've flogged that picture for a few hundred nicker'. Paying no heed to the noise, Orson coolly removed the film from the camera and handed it back to the man, saying 'Go right ahead and sue, you bum.'

The witch-hunt was on. Rehearsals moved to the Royal Court: the box-office faces the street with four auditorium entrances, two on either side, and a staircase leading to the general offices. During a morning rehearsal there was a suspicious glint of reflected light seen in the dress circle. There, sure enough, was another photographer who, on being asked to leave, innocently protested he was a member of the Royal Court Society taking a snapshot for his Aunt Fanny's album. His and everyone else's Aunt Fanny! Anyway, after that, all entrances were locked and even the women cleaners were vetted. Larry was given a key to a side entrance and Joan always arrived accompanied by another member of the cast. We employed our own theatre photographer in order to select and distribute the pictures ourselves. There was a love scene in the play which was carefully directed and, with intuitive prescience, photographed but not distributed. At that period the popular press had gossip diaries supposedly giving facts to their readers of the private lives of famous personalities. Most of these were gleaned by bribery, moral blackmail and a large stretch of the imagination; they were nearly all of a vilifying nature and libel cases were frequent. Small items appeared in print for the first time, innocently denying the probability of a split between the Oliviers. This method of provoking speculation was nearly as vicious as the 'hard facts' and a warning to us that they were waiting to pounce. Larry moved out of Eaton Square to a friend with an ex-directory number; Joan, likewise, left her flat and stayed with a chum. My own telephone rang day and night with persuasive or bullying press, to all of whom I was completely impervious. Knowing even the smallest piece of information might give them a lead I became as cunning, lying and ruthless as they were. The strain was horrible: Larry looked more and more haggard and Joan, not very physically strong, became ill. The opening night of *Rhinoceros*, due to run at the Court for five and a half weeks, drew closer; with everyone's tempers taut some kind of emotional clash blew up between Larry and Orson, culminating in Larry taking over the production for the last few days. The première was odd, to say

30

the least. Despite vigilant scrutiny of first-night ticket applicants, the little theatre seemed to be stiff with narky journalists. To make things more fraught Orson showed up,
having commanded a microphone to be placed in the right-
hand gangway aisle of the tiny dress circle, and throughout
the evening he gave instantaneous lighting cues to the stage
electrician in a stereo hi-fi sotto voce. However the curtain
came down to enthusiastic applause at the appointed time
without any further untoward incident. I tore backstage and
found the small courtyard leading to the stage-door thronged
with eager photographers, but only intimate friends gained
entry to the dressing-rooms. Larry left through the side door
and Joan went quietly through the front entrance without
notice. We scanned the papers next morning: nothing except
wonderful criticisms for the play. This, in itself, was ironic:
normally one hoped for a success to engender press interest—
on this occasion it was almost an embarrassment. The accredited theatre-writers sought interviews which had to be
tactfully declined; even Joan's absence for two nights with a
virus infection managed to escape mention.

It had been running for a number of performances and
we relaxed and breathed freely again. A short-lived respite.
At three minutes past eight one Sunday morning I was
awakened by the ubiquitous Ted Goring whom I had been
fobbing off for weeks. 'How many more times do I have to
say I have nothing to tell you?' I asked wearily. 'Perhaps I
have something to tell *you*,' he riposted. 'Have you heard the
eight o'clock news? Vivien has made an announcement from
America signifying that, regretfully, she is prepared to give
Larry his freedom in order to marry Joan Plowright!' Shouting 'Thank you, very much!' I hung up and promptly dialled
Larry's private number at the flat. It was answered by his
foreign housekeeper who embarked on a long, unintelligible

spiel. Cutting through this I demanded curtly that she went and woke him while I held on. Dreamily I heard him say, 'Ginny, darling, I'm half asleep—can't it wait?' Feeling very sick I told him why it couldn't. 'Oh, Jesus Christ!' wrung from him, but he was alert immediately. I asked where Joan was. He said she was staying with George Devine. I suggested he should warn her and get her out of London immediately; similarly advising him to leave the flat with instructions for the foreign maid to answer his telephone—enough to baffle any reporter. Fortunately it was Sunday and, so far as the press were concerned, we had a few hours in hand. I promised to stay in my own flat to deal with the incoming calls, and we arranged a secret bell system for him to telephone me. Wishing each other luck we hung up.

It wasn't long before the fun started. The only salient enquiry was 'Where can I get hold of Laurence Olivier and Joan Plowright?' Having complete confidence in Larry and the dotty maid, and knowing they all had his get-at-able number anyway, I suggested they tried the flat at the same time denying all knowledge of Joan's whereabouts. Around midday I heard the prearranged telephone signal. Larry had a strange story: shortly after my call he had gone to George's house where they discussed the best place to hide Joan, during which time a number of journalists sat outside the front door asking for an interview with George. They had been told he was still asleep but the problem remained—how to get Joan out of the house to stay with her sister in the country without being observed? It had been solved by scaling the wall at the bottom of the garden and she was driven away under the journalists' very noses. Larry added he would stay where he was for a while because he had rung his own flat which also had press squatters. Although still worried he sounded less tense than earlier since Joan was temporarily out of the lime-

2a

2b

light. Late that night he called again. He had been forced to push his way through reporters on his doorstep, but had spoken to Joan who had arrived without incident. Luckily her understudy had gone on for her when she had been ill and would deputise for her the following night. We agreed it would be better to make an announcement that she was unable to appear due to illness. Nobody would really believe it but the fact that she had missed two performances earlier might add a little credence. And what the hell, anyway! There would be enough trouble without involving her personally.

Nearly all the morning papers carried two contrasting pictures from their files: one of Vivien looking, for once, sad and miserable and the 'joke' sexy photograph of Larry and Joan taken at the first reading of *The Entertainer* three years back when he didn't even know her, but conclusively damning used in its present context. I put the statement out and within quarter of an hour was inundated with calls all asking one thing—where was she? Innocently I suggested numerous places where she *might* be although I swore I had no definite information. The Court, that night, was bedlam with photographers and journalists swarming everywhere and being frustrated. In the next few days their behaviour got worse. Still unable to discover Joan's hide-out, the editors gave instructions that she should be found at all costs—and 'costs' was the operative word. They were all given funds to bribe anybody to get the information: Larry's chauffeur was offered a vast sum, the stage-door keeper and, even, the local barman the same; anyone who had contact with either of them in a menial capacity was offered money. It says a lot that nobody fell for this and let him down. Throughout that week Larry looked grey and drawn and he'd lost pounds in weight. As the weekend approached I became smitten with a bright idea. Obviously seeing myself cast as Cupid I telephoned Carole Delfont, Bernie's enchanting wife, and asked if David and I might borrow their house in West Sussex for the weekend. She immediately agreed and offered to ring her local help to clean while we were there. Hastily I declined her offer with thanks and arranged to pick up the keys under the mat. I then asked Larry if he and Joan would care to join us. He was delighted with the idea and said he would motor down after the show on Saturday night. Meanwhile I ordered a car-hire firm to pick up 'Miss Bennett', my sister's married name, at the end of a Hertfordshire lane late Saturday afternoon.

David and I got to Middleton during the morning and stocked the place with food and drink. My main concern was over laundry. Fresh sheets had been put on the beds in the Delfonts' room for our use; not wishing to embarrass or involve them in any possible publicity, I had purposely omitted to tell Carole we would be having guests and stupidly forgotten to bring any extra sheets. Hoisted on my own arrow I couldn't think where we were going to lay our heads without ultimate detection. Eventually I settled for the children's room who wouldn't be fussy if their sheets were rumpled: it contained masses of dolls and fluffy toys, one cot and a small truckle-bed. Knowing I would have to sleep with my knees under my chin I cheered David up with a drink before telling him he would have to sleep with his legs on the floor.

Joan duly arrived, looking ill, tense and frightened. She told us that 'the boys' had discovered her sister's address and had been keeping an eye on the house in case she should be there. She first saw them when she was sitting in a chair in shadow, unseen herself, and watched them prowl round the garden peering into every room. She crawled on her hands and knees and got upstairs, leaving her sister to cope. Worse, they had paid visits to her parents and intimidated her mother with threats to 'ruin her daughter's career completely unless she divulged her whereabouts' reducing the poor woman to hysteria and nervous prostration. (This inhuman treatment was later reported to the Press Council.) Just before midnight Larry joined us. He, too, looked pretty ghastly but he was in a jaunty mood through having foiled some photographers who had followed his car.

The sun shone brilliantly next morning and we went out for a short walk. Both Larry and Joan were looking very ordinary. Middleton is a village consisting of small shops and a number of semi-residential seaside houses; there were few people in the street but when I stopped to buy some potatoes Larry suddenly panicked in case they should be recognised—highly unlikely in the circumstances but his state of mind was understandable—so we slunk back and stayed in the garden. Much relaxed and happier we returned to the battle-front in a hired car Monday afternoon, sending Joan to her unknown destination.

It had previously been arranged to transfer *Rhinoceros* to the Strand Theatre. Oscar Lewenstein, who was presenting the play, had been perturbed over Larry's earlier reluctance to participate in publicity and had asked me 'what are you going to do about it?' This was prior to Vivien's statement and he need not have worried! On the opening night of the transfer, with Maggie Smith replacing Joan, the foyer, the stage-door and all the upper-circle and gallery entrances were thronged with photographers and reporters. God knows what they thought was going to happen but they seemed to outnumber the audience. Larry had arrived early in the day for a rehearsal and stayed in the theatre but when he, eventually, tried to leave he was surrounded by a clicking horde. Before battling his way through he said, 'Gentlemen, I regret I have nothing to tell you.' Incensed, they swarmed over the car, shouting and rocking it. When he arrived at the flat there was a similar reception committee awaiting him. This human bull-baiting continued, day and night, without let-up. I think it speaks volumes for him that never once did he lose his temper or alter his courteous attitude towards the scandal seekers throughout the whole grisly period. Without doubt he was doing his best to protect both Joan and Vivien, but at enormous personal cost to himself. He told me the divorce proceedings had been put into motion but, with luck, he would be in America during the hearing. They were both going; he to appear in *Becket* and Joan in *A Taste of Honey*. In the spring of the following year he sent a very funny letter describing his nuptials. In order to avoid any more publicity they went to a Judge in a strange place called Norwalk to get a special licence; from there they were directed to a tiny hamlet called Wilton. Having given two official maiden ladies his name they seriously enquired his 'profession' and 'had he been married before?' Fortified by this flash of serendipity Larry and Joan proceeded to a little village green and discovered—above a drugstore—a Justice of the Peace who, apologising for his secretary's absence (he was ski-ing because it was St. Patrick's Day!), pronounced them, within the space of two minutes, man and wife. For a bit this new nomenclature threw their hotel staff who, playing it safe, addressed Joan as Sir Lady Olivier. While they were in the States a number of eminent people, led by Penelope Gilliatt, successfully campaigned against the methods the popular press were using to extract information and the original format of the social diaries was changed—in the case of the *Daily Mail* even the name was altered from Paul Tanfield to Charles Greville.

2

Chichester: An exciting experiment

BEFORE going to America Larry had bought a house in a much-coveted Regency terrace in Brighton. Not entirely content with the architect's interior layout he left comprehensive instructions with his factotum to translate to builders certain quite simple labour-saving devices. That these in practice were tantamount to rebuilding the house, not to mention doubling the original purchase price, appeared to have escaped him; and eighteen months later the workmen were still having a ball. When Larry and Joan arrived back from New York they were forced to stay in an hotel adjoining the house. He telephoned me and invited us down for the weekend. They were radiantly happy and, with great pride, Larry told us that Joan was expecting a baby in some months' time. During the evening he told us he was going to run a summer season at Chichester. I thought, at first, he'd gone mad and meant a concert party and, as he explained the idea, I still thought he was mad. He told us that a man called Leslie Evershed-Martin had seen an excerpt on television from the open-stage theatre in Stratford, Ontario which had filled him with ambition to build a similar one in Sussex. He had somehow persuaded some business acquaintances to put up some money, the local Council to grant a peppercorn-rent site in a park, an architect to take a gamble and a building firm prepared to accept long-term payment. Larry had received a letter in America giving him all these details and asking if he would become the Director. I personally thought the possibility of his refusing had never entered their pretty little heads and was slightly stunned when he asked me if I would care to tackle it. I said 'You must be joking' and dismissed it. But after dinner he started again. In moving tones he told me the reasons for his acceptance: a brand new theatre inspired by faith and the money supplied by voluntary funds from the public. He elaborated and told me there would be endless fund-raising schemes—and committee meetings—and 'a lovely few weeks in the summer'. Again he asked me to consider it. It sounded a masochist's paradise, but not for me. Next evening, at home, the lovely monster telephoned. With a hangover, and certainty that he always got his own way, I heard myself agreeing. The following week I went down to Chichester, ostensibly to be vetted by Mr. Evershed-Martin, and met Larry at the site which was a muddy hole in the ground swarming with workmen. He regarded it with love and awe, much as one of the Pharaohs might have regarded the sands in the desert when the pyramids were being built. Heaven proved him right about those ghastly committee meetings. They were convened at least once a fortnight at Chichester, Worthing, London, Brighton and Lancing. Why, I asked myself, always in the dining-room smelling slightly of stale food? Larry was seldom present—he has an antipathy towards them—consequently the Board, erroneously, thought they were dealing with a very easy-going man. But he attended one in

Chichester and sat apparently oblivious to the vital issues being debated: the prices to be charged for ice-cream, post-cards and souvenirs. He sat, half asleep, impervious to the buzz of conversation, until a technical question regarding the theatre itself came under discussion. He waited while the members talked between themselves before he uttered; then in a couple of sentences, in a very quiet voice, he made it crystal clear that any matters relating to the professional side of the building must be referred to him and he would give them his decision. It was said most charmingly but with great authority and received in stunned silence. Glancing at his watch, he announced he would drive me back to Brighton and left. Thereafter polite battle was given between all the enthusiastic amateurs versus the professionals. One argument developed over the bells in the foyer which are sounded in a normal theatre to warn the audience when the curtain is about to rise. In Chichester this presented a problem due to it being situated in the middle of a park. It was presumed, rightly, that they might stroll around the grounds or go to the little pub at the end of the drive-in and an ordinary bell would not be heard. The Founder had brought some curious cow-bells as souvenirs of Greece: they were large circles of spokes with bells attached on the ends and had to be manually, and energetically, turned before they gaily chimed—not exactly practical! Larry found the solution: to tape his own voice and amplify it all over the grounds. One of his more endearing aspects at this time was his preoccupation with an idea he'd thought up years earlier with Ralph Richardson, namely that if ever he should have a new theatre he would launch a rocket from the roof on the opening night which would be seen for miles, to be known as 'Ralph's Rocket'. This became obsessional and endless journeys were made by me to pyrotechnic firms who were eager at first but damp squibs when

39

they heard its purpose. They patiently pointed out that it might fall and set fire to the surrounding trees, houses or cars in the car-park; could cause a sudden demise through shock or, at best, summon out the local lifeboat. Told all this Larry reluctantly accepted his defeat but went around with a nasty long face for quite a while.

When the theatre idea was first mooted some of the Cicestrians were dead against it. Groups were sharply divided between bring-and-buy-coffee-mornings-at-all-costs and we-don't-want-it-whatever-it-costs, which led to many delightful hot arguments when scandal and gossip palled. In the autumn we went into a restaurant after a session at the theatre. Very few people recognise Larry offstage, he has acquired a 'faceless' exterior and is shorter than one imagines. Suddenly we heard the name Olivier coming from a table of local big-wigs tucking in on expense accounts. 'Olivier? Yer mean the actor chap who made a film with a dem good battle in it?' 'I hear he's at the bottom of that white elephant up in the park.' 'Bit of a comedown, eh? Suppose he can't get anything better to do.' This last epitome of wit was greeted by hearty guffaws and Larry slowly turned and stared at them. There was an embarrassed silence, followed by a call for the bill. As they shuffled out one of them whispered 'It couldn't have been the feller himself, could it?' Highly amused Larry turned to me: 'There you are, Ginny, my public image. I wonder which dem film he saw.'

I went to the hotel for a meeting with Larry and found him in a state of justifiable hopping rage. The previous day two men had appeared on the doorstep of his house. They rang the bell, which was answered by a workman, and said they'd come to take some measurements. In good faith they were admitted; but they had then proceeded, not to take measurements, but photographs and notes of the house for the *Daily Express*. Through sheer accident and Larry's own elephant mind—which never forgets *anything*—he had seen them, and recognised one of them. He challenged him immediately and, quite correctly, warned him he could be sued for illegal entry but that he would not pursue this provided nothing relating to him or the house appeared in the paper. He had then telephoned the *Express* and registered his strong disapproval of their methods. This news was ill-timed for me, to say the least, because I had arranged to try and persuade him to be photographed for the first time in the grounds of the theatre. This little operation had been wished on me via Lord Bessborough: his secretary had a boy friend who 'took pictures' and wanted some of Larry. It had been stressed that he could see all the shots and approve or can them, but the photographer wished to try and get one printed in a paper. Faced with the prior debacle it needed everything I'd got to talk him into this. For the sake of the theatre he agreed. We drove down to Chichester a few days later and Larry was marvellously co-operative. The results were sent to me and he only vetoed two. Three days later one of these appeared in the *Daily Mail*. Understandably the secretary, Larry and I were all livid with this breach of promise. I was requested to unravel it and discovered the very attractive boy friend was a highly skilful French photographer who had sold the picture not only in England but all over the Continent. Blast; you really can't win.

When a building has reached the topmost stage of its development, i.e. the roof, it has become traditional to hold a 'topping-out' ceremony. This was scheduled to take place in November and a date was fixed to mark the occasion. Television, the national press and all the local press were alerted of the event and the responses were splendid. It was agreed that I should travel to Brighton on an early train and pick up Larry at the hotel. I arrived, just after nine, and went up to the suite. Joan told me he had just got into the bath and I heard a voice shouting 'Why the devil are you so early? Have some coffee. I'll come and join you in a minute.' He did, about half an hour later. The ceremony was timed for noon. I asked how long it would take us by car, he replied between forty-five to fifty minutes, so I relaxed. At ten-thirty we left the hotel and he decided to pop into the new house, which was virtually next door, to have a quick word with a workman who was baffled by his instructions to have a 'private drawer' fixed in his cupboard in the bathroom. This was Larry's own invention and he had spent hours drawing it mathematically to scale, but for some reason the clarity of the design did not convey itself to the carpenter. Larry immediately went into action and started to 'produce' the poor man. Explaining quietly and carefully, he took him step by step over the plans. Eventually a great light seemed to dawn on the gentleman and mutual congratulations were exchanged. At the same time a great light dawned on me that we were going to be late if we did not leave very soon. I muttered this and rather reluctantly he agreed to go. We walked round the house to the garage in the mews and got into the car. There was a slight oath, which meant he was out of petrol, and we made for a garage. The nearest one was closed so we drove into the town and filled up. By now it was apparent to him that we were going to be pressed for time and in a strange tone he asked me to fasten the safety belt and hoped I did not mind speed. I did, but there was no point in saying so at that moment. He looked at his watch and informed me that we could make it in thirty-three minutes. I said I prayed so—and meant it. The car was a Jaguar and the coastal road turns and bends the entire way. He strapped himself in and put his foot on the accelerator and we were practically airborne.

He then proceeded to give me an admonitory lecture for, as he put it, letting him in for making a public appearance at the forthcoming ceremony. Why should he have to face the press? Why be photographed? Why meet a lot of people he didn't want to meet? And he would not make a speech and the whole thing was my fault! I feebly tried to point out that it happened to be part of his responsibilities and it was primarily for the workmen's benefit who had been working strenuously in order to try and get his theatre ready on time. This seemed to have a temporarily calming effect until I unwisely told him he would have to drink a glass of beer or sherry to toast them. Immediately the wrath was turned on again. For God's sake couldn't I remember that he was on a diet and that meant the waggon and he wasn't going to upset his routine to please anybody! Knowing my Larry far too well by now, I replied I thought it might be a good thing if he concentrated for a moment on what he was going to say. That was received in silence which continued for the next few miles, during which time I began pondering over the events of the morning. I knew he suffered from intense nerves, but he had known well in advance about the topping-out and it had met with his whole-hearted approval; I had arrived in plenty of time, why then had he apparently deliberately made us so late? I started wondering how his mind worked and I believe his thought process is very simple although I am quite sure it is unconscious: when he has to take any major decision a minor one is substituted and the secondary problem is given his whole concentration. I had seen an example that morning: the conversation with the carpenter that could have waited a few more hours, the petrol that could have been checked and dealt with by a telephone call. I remembered back to other occasions when he had applied the same technique as if for self-protection. In my own mind I christened it 'toothpaste', meaning to me that when everything gets on top of you and is all too big, it becomes essential that you should acquire a certain brand of toothpaste on Thursday afternoon when all the shops are closed. I prayed we would soon arrive. A signpost told us we were four miles away from Chichester and Larry put on a final burst of speed and with the horn sounding we arrived at the site just as the cathedral clock chimed midday.

I saw a large crowd of press and television cameras and a very anxious Mr. Evershed-Martin waiting to greet us. Remembering that I had a job to perform I unfastened the belt which had held me in such good stead, took a deep breath to give me courage for the ordeal, opened the door to step out and ignominiously collapsed on the ground in a heap. I had been so scared on the journey that my limbs had gone numb and I had no strength left—nor any dignity neither. The Founder gave me a very odd look and helped me to my feet. He greeted Larry with overt relief and together we made our way into the half-finished theatre. It was a most beautiful autumn day with the sun's rays pouring from the open roof onto the raised slabs of concrete which were to hold the seats. The stage itself was a gaping void, the steel structures in the auditorium were exposed and it looked very lovely and very vulnerable. I think some of these emotions must have chased through Larry's mind because his mood changed within seconds. He was affable, excited and exuded charm to everyone. There were two distinct groups of people, the larger one round a microphone consisting of the Board, their families and friends, plus press, photographers and some local enthusiasts: on the other side were

44

the workmen surreptitiously sipping glasses of beer and shuffling self-consciously. Poor loves, I thought, I bet you, too, are a little apprehensive. After some informal chat it was proposed that Larry should ascend the ladder leading up to the summit of the roof. He asked me to accompany him and at the base there was a table with drinks. I enquired innocently if he would prefer beer or sherry, to which he replied 'sherry'. He started to scale the ladder and I followed with the drink in my hand. Once up there he gave not only a wonderful and sincere speech but endeared each one of the tough workmen to him for life. After he had finished they sang, quite spontaneously, 'For he's a jolly good fellow' and I knew that, yet again, all would be well from my angle. This proved right, because not only did he pose for dozens of pictures but he gave interviews to the press and also to television. While the latter was being set up I was highly amused to hear him ask if there was a little whisky around and to see him drink it with obvious enjoyment. Two hours later he made his apologies for leaving, and as we walked to the car he said 'Ginny, I've been a perfect bastard to you. I'm sorry, my darling, I don't mean it and you know it.' Of course he had but I understood him and why he did it and instantly forgave him.

His attitude towards the press generally has been one of complete distrust over a period of many years. I once asked him what fired it off originally, and he told me that when he was appearing in New York, long before the war, he was asked by an American columnist if he did not believe that Katharine Cornell, the First Lady of the American theatre, was the greatest living actress. He replied that, although he thought Miss Cornell a very *fine* actress, he could not subscribe to her being 'the greatest' because England had quite a number of superb actresses such as Edith Evans, Flora

Robson and Peggy Ashcroft. Next morning the paper had banner headlines to the effect that 'Unknown British Actor Thinks Cornell Stinks'. This, understandably, infuriated him and he vowed to himself he would never give another interview. Naturally the promise was an impossible one to keep but it soured his mind towards the press for a very long time, culminating in the pitiless behaviour to which he had been subjected so recently.

In January the plans for the first Chichester season were announced. Larry's choice of plays had caused many long hours of research and discussion and interminable hours of reading. Eventually he decided on a virtually unknown Jacobean comedy, *The Chances*, which he unearthed at the British Museum; an obscure Jacobean tragedy, *The Broken Heart*, and Chekhov's *Uncle Vanya*. These were planned as different examples of using the open stage. The cast read like 'Who's Who': Laurence Olivier, Sybil Thorndike, Michael Redgrave, Joan Greenwood, Lewis Casson, Joan Plowright, John Neville, Fay Compton, Keith Michell, Rosemary Harris, Athene Seyler, Kathleen Harrison, Andrew Morell. The general reaction to this was the stress laid on age—one bright journalist making the aggregate into many hundreds of years. Rehearsals were scheduled to commence in the spring, first in London and the remaining weeks in Chichester. This presented a billeting problem. Chichester, then, had very few hotels geared to accommodate theatre people and virtually no residents prepared to lease their own homes for the season. During the preliminary months I had been working down there I had come across a delightful private hotel called Woodend, a few miles outside the city. At one time it had been occupied by Admiral

Hardy of 'kiss me!' fame. It nestles at the foot of the Downs with acres of gardens, woods, views and peace and quiet. It is owned by Elizabeth Broad, a General's daughter who runs it with her deliciously scatty Polish partner. I thought it might be the ideal retreat for the Oliviers: it was so tucked away the locals couldn't direct one to it, so I doubted if the press would find it. I invited Larry and Joan to luncheon to test his reaction. The two owners took infinite trouble with the menu and we awaited their arrival, timed for one o'clock. By a quarter-to-two I was a trifle anxious and telephoned Brighton. A fraught Larry told me Joan had been out shopping, had only just got back, but they would be on their way. With many apologies I reported this to the two ladies who airily told me there was nothing to worry about. I only thought if I'd been cooking a Lucullan banquet to impress people who were two hours late I *certainly* would be worried. They arrived shortly after three o'clock, were instantly taken with the laissez-faire charm of the place and arranged to lease a wing (necessary for the newly-born son and the nanny) before departing. Incidentally, the lunch was superb—I wish I'd been born Polish. That evening I dined with 'the family' who, naturally, were delighted with the day's outcome. They went on at great length telling me of their plans to start a stud-farm—I wasn't too sure what it meant—and, for commencement, had imported a Polish stallion called Fruckt. Even to me the scheme became clear ... Throughout the long horsey dinner I listened politely and told them Larry would be *very* interested. Why? God knows! It was simply something to say.

The first reading and get-together of the company took place at a church hall in Chelsea for *The Chances*. It was all very thrilling and exciting. Everyone felt they were pioneers and upstaged each other in protestations of non-caring what they did or played. They consumed quarts of coffee and developed instant brother-love. Larry gave a magnificent welcoming speech which was funny and inspiring at the same time. He introduced everybody to everyone, forgetting their names but heavily prompted by Pieter Rogers, the Chichester general manager. Later in the week was the date fixed for the official press pre-view at the theatre. It was May and the English weather was at its best. The sun was hot, birds were billing and cooing and the brashness of the unconventional design of the building was camouflaged by the green trees and the warmth of the countryside. It had been built on a shoestring, there were insufficient dressing-rooms, non-existent wing space and—heaven alone knew later—not enough lavatories, but the sun shone, God was in His heaven and all was well in the theatre world. One tiny exception, the size of a greenfly, marred the harmony: the Founder, without consultation, had accepted a local rose-grower's offer and masses of multi-coloured blooms were flourishing on a triangle of concrete abutting the foyer. This, to the extreme disapproval of Philip Powell, the architect, who claimed it ruined the symmetry of his design.

For the remaining weekends before moving down to Chichester, Larry called the small cast of *Uncle Vanya* for Sunday rehearsals in the theatre to accustom them to playing a quiet, concentrated play on the open stage. These sessions were closely guarded to discourage the public from walking into the auditorium on the excuse that 'they'd given their money and had every right to know what was going on'. In Chelsea there is a successful restaurant run by two actors, John Glen and David Enders, which Larry sometimes frequented, and he arranged with them to operate the

Theatre Restaurant when the season opened. Princess Margaret and Lord Snowdon were occasional patrons and dined there one Saturday night. The new theatre was the subject of the after-dinner conversation and Lord Snowdon, with keen interest, expressed a desire to view it. David Enders telephoned me to enquire if it would be possible to show the Royal visitors round the following day. I explained I didn't think it would be feasible as it was a working day for the company but I would contact Larry. He was very perturbed owing to the tight working schedule; he had given Michael Redgrave some hours off, but uppermost in his mind was the breaking of his rule of never allowing anyone into a rehearsal and he was much against the idea. With slight embarrassment I retailed this to David Enders but it became obvious that it was too late to cancel it. Next morning I gave Larry the answer and he asked me to be present. It was teeming with rain and the small cast arrived in offbeat working gear. Larry summoned them to his dressing-room and told them of the visit, adding that he would arrange with a little public house on the corner to serve them tea about three o'clock. Some of the company were rather downcast at this dismissal but accepted the edict as part of the regime. As it neared three o'clock the cast were dismissed, Larry and Laurier Lister, his assistant, remained in the auditorium and I was detailed to stand in the glass-surrounded foyer to await the arrival. A car drew into the waterlogged drive and four occupants got out. Feeling apprehensive and pretty stupid, I unlocked the glass door and helped the visitors over the damp concrete planked with wood to the steps leading up to the auditorium. Larry oozed icy charm and introduced Her Royal Highness and Lord Snowdon to Laurier Lister. Earlier he had had qualms that Lord Snowdon might photograph the theatre in his professional

49

capacity. He need not have worried: only Princess Margaret had a camera slung round her neck which she used with consummate ease. Both of them showed great enthusiasm for the building, particularly the Princess who bravely climbed the spiral stairs to the top acting level. This is a small area of a few square feet; it was unfinished without any bars to protect it. She walked to the edge and stood, hundreds of feet above us, commenting on the view. They were intrigued by the sound box, a comparatively new innovation, which Lord Snowdon was quick to appreciate and they both experimented with it. Taking her leave, the Princess expressed her regret that she had not seen any rehearsal or Olivier directing. With a twinkle he replied that Her Royal Highness's reputation for mimicry was well known and he was loth to add to her repertoire. At this point there was a diversion: out of the darkness emerged a slightly exhilarated figure; Michael Redgrave who had just come from the secret wedding of his daughter Vanessa to Tony Richardson. He looked very startled when introduced to the Princess, half imagining she had joined the cast of *Uncle Vanya*. The royal party left; the cast returned; work was resumed.

The Chichester invasion weekend arrived. Larry with Joan, the baby and nanny, had made arrangements to move into Woodend during Saturday afternoon, but when the V.I.P's arrived there was no one *literally* to receive them. They had gone to a horse show some miles distant and had taken the entire staff to look after their Very Important Ponies, leaving Sir Laurence to heave his not inconsiderable luggage upstairs unaided. He didn't appear to mind or to be surprised, which was maybe just as well because their hours were casual and his became arduous if not frankly bizarre.

On Monday morning the whole company assembled in the

foyer of the theatre to have a glass of champagne and meet the Board. Leslie Evershed-Martin, the Founder, welcomed the company and said that he was now handing over the theatre to Larry and the professionals and expressed his regret that the building was two months behind schedule. Larry responded: he gravely thanked the Board for passing the theatre over to him, adding that he felt sure they would understand if he, in his turn, was two months behind schedule with the first production. There were gales of laughter from the company. The Board stood in horrified silence. People who don't know are apt to take Larry seriously and the Chichester Board never really cottoned on to his wicked sense of fun. The cast dispersed into the auditorium. It suddenly hit me that I myself had not got an office in which to work. I mentioned it to dear Jim Battersby, one of the Board members, who had a factory very near the town centre. Within half an hour I was installed there in one of the director's rooms with a switchboard, a private line, and I was in business. Soon journalists and photographers were making the trip down to Chichester to write 'the story of the birth of the theatre'. Interviews took place in the ultra-modern factory and even that did not appear unusual but rather part of the pioneering spirit of the whole venture.

To allow the actors all available time to get used to the feel of the new stage I concentrated my efforts on the people behind the idea, explaining that Larry was too occupied with the work to be spared. This happened to be true at the time, but it was a reason I was forced to use on hundreds of occasions. He was still obsessively chary of giving any interviews at all. He gave us a company lecture instilling in us that there were certain extra-mural activities we were bound to undertake, the most important being a Commemoration Ceremony in the cathedral. It was a special service, conducted by the Bishop, Dr. Roger Wilson, for the company and various people who had been responsible for organising the funds and the building of the theatre. The sun blazed down and it was amusing to watch the company assembling outside the cathedral. Most of them appeared ill-at-ease as if they hadn't been inside a church for a very long time. They obviously had not got together sartorially—some were for Ascot, some in mourning and some for tennis—but all wearing highly unsuitable headgear. Inside the cathedral it was cool and quiet with slanting rays falling from the stained glass windows. The clergy filed in: choristers, deacons, the Dean, the Bishop, the full panoply of the Church. The Bishop's address was based on the parallel between the church and the stage. Both, he said, made a direct appeal to the senses and the emotions and, from the senior building, he welcomed and blessed the newcomers. It was simple, direct and very moving. On the way out one of the non-Protestant Board members said to Larry with great enthusiasm: 'A lovely sermon, Larry, a truly lovely sermon!' To which he replied, looking round at all his company, 'My dear chap, I'm only amazed the rafters did not fall on our heads!'

Meantime rehearsals continued with workmen hammering, scenery being painted on the foyer floor, and casual strollers from the park wandering in to see what was going on. It was total bedlam and one day Larry lost his temper and sent for some of the Board members to protest. He was justified in one way because he was unable to work under those conditions and his reputation was at stake. There was enormous international interest in Chichester and there were a great number of people who were longing for him to fail. On the other hand it was vitally necessary to finish the building. The choice was between comfort for the customers and the quality of the goods they were paying to see. After hours of argument a compromise was agreed on: the cast would rehearse as late as possible in the theatre and the workmen would receive double pay and work through the night. By now the effort was beginning to show in Larry's face and his temper was tetchy, except with the company whom he treated with infinite patience and understanding.

One weekend we were all four, Larry, Joan, my husband David, and myself, lying out in the gardens sun-bathing. Larry was a few yards away immersed in concocting some programme notes, applying his escape technique 'toothpaste' again, and the three of us were idly chatting. Joan told us that the National Theatre had approached Larry to become its first Director. We asked what his reactions were. She replied that he didn't really want to do it but he couldn't think of anyone else so he thought he'd better have a go. We discussed the merits and demerits for a while and Larry came over and joined us. He said he had been thinking and talking about it for a long time but had not yet completely made up his mind. One aspect of the job made him anxious to accept: the idea of forming and training a regular Company—not just star actors but building up talented unknown ones—and forming an ensemble that would be famous for the name *of* the Company and not necessarily the names *in* the Company. This he felt he could and should do. At the same time he knew it would be a hard task-master and he expressed doubts of his ability to carry out the grave responsibility but remarked philosophically that as he was one of the leading actors he supposed he could make a balls-up as well as anybody else. We pointed out also that it would curtail his own activities as an actor in other media and he agreed, saying wryly that even a famous one had to pay his rent.

David and I had taken to visiting the Horse and Groom, a tiny unspoilt pub in a neighbouring village and we got up and started to walk away. We were asked 'Where the hell are you going?' 'To have a drink,' we answered. 'Not without me!' came the reply. It is a good two-mile walk through the woods and we were all gasping by the time we arrived. I don't think Larry had been into a public house for years and he was delighted with it. It is mostly frequented by the local farm workers and nearby inhabitants. After a couple of drinks he entered into a learned conversation with a farm-hand about pig-breeding. In no time they were standing each other a drink. When we left cheery farewells were called after us and Larry said how much he had enjoyed himself. It became a regular habit of ours to ask each other 'Going down the wood?' and I think these little sessions did a lot to unwind him. On one occasion, when word had got around that he was Laurence Olivier, one of his pub mates retailed this to him with great solemnity and said 'I told Fred not to talk daft. After all, I said, you've seen him in here yerself, he's no fuckin' actor!' Larry gravely agreed, thanked him for the defence and bought him a pint.

We were three weeks off the opening night and preparations were reaching fever pitch. When G.P.O. engineers were installing the office telephones I was highly amused by one of them poking his head into my room saying 'If you're Missus Fairweather, Miss, there's a Mister 'Arold 'Obson wanting you—you can take 'im down our tempo'ry.' Running out to the drive I lay on my stomach and talked to Harold with builders' lorries whipping by, missing me by inches. A cluster of pre-fabricated huts had been erected as an office block and a restaurant unit was assembled adjoining the theatre. Everything possible was being done to try and make up the two months' time lag with the building but it was clear that tempers were getting very dodgy due to tiredness and over work. One afternoon Larry called me into his dressing-room, which he also used as an office, and said, 'Ginny, we're in one hell of a jam. What would you do if I told you we couldn't open?' There really was no answer to give and he explained to me that we were in dire trouble with the local fire officials. It appears that when the original plans were submitted to the Council, it either had not become clear to them or through ignorance of the Licensing Regulations someone omitted to point out that there was no safety curtain to prevent fire spreading, as in proscenium theatres. As it was virtually the first theatre of its kind to be built in this country with an open stage there was no precedent to fall back on and we were truly in trouble. An emergency meeting of the Building Committee had been called for that night and he said he would let me know the result when he came back to the hotel later. Naturally this information was top secret. The meeting was an indecisive one but Jim Battersby, my ex-host of the factory office, had some suggestions that he proposed putting up to the authorities the following day. After long discussions the ideas were finally accepted but they involved a certain amount of structural alteration. Extra fire escape exits had to be made, the close-fitted carpet covering the huge foyer had to be taken up and substituted by a special flooring. This would entail not only more expense which could be ill-afforded, but for the next two vital weeks the place would be infested with workmen throughout the day and night. Larry called the company together and told them the whole story since it would affect every department, actors, scenery, lighting and costumes. He enjoined us all to keep it to ourselves and work even harder under almost impossible conditions. From then on it was chaos but a curious spirit of being part of the fight became apparent in the workmen. They knew Larry and the company had their troubles and they did their level best to hammer softly—if such a thing is possible. The worst blasting of the large concrete triangle carrying out the hexagonal design flanking the foyer was timed for the evening and the cast went over to the restaurant to continue rehearsing. Philip Powell, the architect, and Mr. Evershed-Martin watched the demolition. Although sorry to see part of his design destroyed I think he was privately pleased that Mr. Evershed-Martin's roses would also have to be sacrificed.

The next day was scheduled for a *Vanya* rehearsal and there was a break in the call sheet from five to six o'clock with instructions that everyone should stay in the theatre. Promptly at five o'clock Larry left, to return ten minutes later with some strange men. He entered from the top entrance, which is the most impressive view of the whole theatre, and slowly walked down the stairs until he reached the stage level. With due ceremony he introduced Dame Sybil Thorndike, Lady Olivier, Sir Michael Redgrave, Sir Lewis Casson, and invited them to follow him and the unknown gentlemen for a drink in the restaurant. Sybil, with a really naughty wink, whispered to me as she went by 'Oh, I know what Larry is up to, clever boy!' I thought he was too. Being confronted with those Knights and Ladies of the theatre for the first time (all of them oozing 'helplessness' and charm) would have overpowered most people. The cast returned to the theatre and Larry stayed behind to assure the gentlemen that all their conditions would be carried out provided he had their assurance that the season could open as planned. This they promised to give—after the work had been done. I wish I had been present during his appeal, I am sure that more than a hint of Henry V at Agincourt must have crept in.

When he came back we all plied him with questions. He cursed the poor architect for not having foreseen the snag, and then the whole of Chichester starting with the fire authorities. He was deadly serious but incredibly funny and, though sorry for his concern, we couldn't help laughing at him. It was a very ham performance.

He decided to break for the day and asked one of the stage management to get in some beer for the workmen. Michael, Joan and I went down to his dressing-room and had a drink. He suddenly suggested we all went out to the town and got tight. Joan, who was not drinking, demurred mildly, pointing out that he would have a headache in the morning to which he replied that it could not possibly be any worse than the one he'd already got. We went to a small club-restaurant run by one of the first woman television inter-viewers, Joan Griffiths, which had the off-putting name of The Curry Club. Her own stage experience had accustomed her to the odd hours theatre people kept and she put herself out to keep open for our convenience. The four of us were practically the only customers, luckily, as the conversation became very heated and personal. Larry, illogically, now blamed the Board and the builders for the situation. Possibly inadequate funds were the original cause of the delay in the building but the same position would inevitably have arisen although it would have been discovered earlier. Unfortunately none of these arguments would shake Larry's conviction that he was dealing with incompetent fools. He himself is a perfectionist and has little patience with any-thing or anyone who does not measure up to his own standards. Eventually we left after Larry had apologised to Joan Griffiths for keeping her up late and grumbled some apologies to Michael and me. We dropped Michael at his rented house in the town and Joan, who had not drunk anything, drove us back to the hotel. I had a final drink with him in his suite and muttering that he was every sort of no good bastard, he went to bed.

Some evenings later he confided to me that Joan was expecting another baby. She was only a few months pregnant, but her role in *The Chances* demanded a long and swift chase all round the various tiers of the theatre. The doctors had come to the conclusion that this might prove too strenuous and it had been arranged for one of the girls in the company to double for her at that moment. I was asked to keep it quiet, not for any other reason than that it might detract from the plays in which she was going to take part. Sensibly Larry explained that if it were known, many members of the audience would speculate on her figure and worry about her being on the stage 'in her condition'. Also he did not want to see a lot of women counting on their fingers whenever she appeared, adding the actors would be forced to look at a number of ugly thighs without a lot of tick-tacking to further distract them. Mind you, it didn't prevent him telling everyone he met—he was so proud. Another member of the company, Gene Anderson, who died tragically three years later, was expecting her first baby and had originally been cast as a young virgin in the second play *The Broken Heart*. Her role was reluctantly taken from her. As Larry remarked sadly, 'Young—indubitably, a virgin? Don't be bloody silly! What the hell is the matter with this place—it should be called Fertility and Fecundity!'

Tuesday, July 3rd was the first performance with two dress rehearsals prior to the première. Applications for tickets for the opening night were phenomenal: the theatre seats 1,360 and it could have been sold many times over. During the last few days the weather had changed but Tuesday morning dawned with brilliant sunshine that continued throughout the day. It became known ironically as 'Founder's Weather'. Hectic last minute preparations were in progress down at the theatre; television cameras were everywhere in evidence and national, international and local photographers. The workshop was some distance from the theatre in a large and ugly disused public house—The Unicorn—which was ideal for the purpose. It had ample space for the wardrobe, property department and dyeing rooms and it was possible to accommodate staff in the living quarters at the top of the pub. One disadvantage was the difficulty of transporting equipment between it and the theatre. A lorry was available for the heavy stuff, but it became a commonplace sight to see an actor driving his car surrounded by costumes or bicycling actresses with props strapped on their handlebars. Throughout the morning these processions were scurrying back and forth across the car park adjoining the theatre delivering wigs, costumes and props that had needed final alterations after the previous night's rehearsal. There were queues besieging the box office, whilst inside a run-through of *The Chances* was being held. In my own department I was as nervous as a cat. I had got two hundred critics and journalists arriving shortly, representing the world press. I had organised their accommodation, ordered a private bus to transport some to the various hotels, and made sure they would have sufficient telephone lines at their disposal to ring back their notices and coverage of the occasion. My office was the largest in the block and I had asked the theatre bar to deliver a quantity of drink for the intervals. Checking through the arrangements in my mind before going back to Woodend to change, I suddenly realised that, even with the help of my husband and my assistant, Richard Walton (stage-designer Tony Walton's younger brother), I couldn't cope with the 'bar' and answer the innumerable questions I knew I would be asked. I remembered that the Earl of Bessborough's warm-hearted and amusing wife, Mary, had earlier offered her services in any practical way. I grabbed the telephone and told her my dilemma. Down the other end of the line came her rich American drawl assuring me that I could have George, her valued Italian butler, for the evening on one tiny condition —that they could bring their friends over to my room for interval drinks in preference to queueing for hours at the one and only bar. 'The deal's on' I said and went off to change, feeling I had done everything within my power to ensure that the press angle would go smoothly.

I returned within an hour and went backstage to wish everyone well. There was an electric tension in all the rooms. Although actors are reputed to be totally selfish and egocentric, I truly believe that that night everybody was praying the evening would go well for Larry's sake. They all knew how much he himself had put into the venture and how much his reputation was at stake. I wandered over to my own office feeling tense with nervous excitement. Within a short while the press started to arrive, some bringing with them the London evening papers carrying the announcement that Larry had been appointed the first Director of the National Theatre. This, by itself, was heady stuff and heightened the expectancy of the evening. Mary Bessborough's dear George was already installed behind a hastily assembled bar dispensing hospitality with Latin charm and tact. Soon the room was full to bursting point. A small paved area outside the office had two opulent cars parked on it blocking the entrance to the press room. I asked Richard to find the owners and ask them to remove the vehicles. The reply came back that they belonged to members of the Board who considered they were 'privileged' to leave them there and had no intention of moving them. More press arrived and had to spread into the grounds. Alan Brien and Bernard Levin teased me about the obstruction my private car park was causing. I told them who the owners were and they said in that case the inconveniences should be put to good use. This everyone proceeded to do and before long the car tops were covered with dirty glasses and cigarette stubs. During this Larry came into the office to wish me luck. With an air of psychotic calm, he sought me out and, as he kissed me, he said he was sorry to butt in. 'I expect these are all your friends.' 'They are' I replied. 'The press!' 'Christ!' he said and vanished.

As it neared the moment for the non-existent curtain to rise, more and more people thronged into the press room including two dear little Japanese—a critic and his photographer—who had flown in from Tokyo that morning. True to our bargain Lord and Lady Bessborough brought their own house guests, including Peter and Carla Thorneycroft and the French Ambassador and his wife. Five minutes before the 'off' Olivier's dulcet tones, accompanied by a fanfare of trumpets, echoed round Oaklands Park urging the audience, with enormous politeness, to take their seats. The last trumpet sounded and the three-year-old vision had become a reality.

Back in the office we all set to and washed hundreds of dirty glasses in buckets of water brought over from the bar as there was no running water on the premises. The first act was quite short and it seemed no time at all before the interval was upon us. A tall, elegant figure in a white dinner jacket with red cummerbund swayed over to the press room: Kenneth Tynan who was writing for the *Observer*. Accepting a drink he smiled acidly 'Am-m-musing little romp' and turned away to chat to his colleagues.

I went into the theatre for the last half of the play. The

audience were enjoying themselves and consequently so were the cast. As the applause started I left my seat and went back to the office to prepare for any critics who wished to use the telephones. The plans for the rest of the night were a public firework display in the park and a private party in the restaurant, given by the two actors running it, for the company, their friends, and the Board. Leslie Evershed-Martin had asked my husband to invent a slogan for the set-piece of the fireworks to 'light the sky as a glorious finale'. After many hilarious, if not slanderous, suggestions they had chosen 'The Chances Are You'll Come Again', which seemed to strike an optimistic note. To the distant accompaniment of bangs and explosions the press were busily writing and telephoning their notices. Richard Walton, who had been back in the theatre, put his head round the door and said I should pop over, there was a bit of trouble. That was the biggest understatement of the evening: the foyer was pandemonium. Word had got round that there was to be a party and most of the audience had assumed they were to be included. The doors were locked from inside to prevent the hundreds of firework spectators from entering and it seemed an impossibility to clear the mob in the foyer. Poor Pieter Rogers, trying to make himself heard over the din, was petulant and almost crying, imploring them to go home. But the 'carnival spirit' had got into them and they were barracking and chanting. Somehow order was restored and the disappointed crowd were pushed into the park. I went backstage and met Larry in one of the crowded dressing-rooms. He turned and asked me where the booze was for the restaurant party because he had run out. I replied I didn't know—where should it be? I was swiftly detailed off to find out. The theatre bar was firmly closed and the restaurant had not received anything, in fact nobody seemed to know anything about it and quite obviously someone had slipped up. Great! I thought. That is all we need to complete the entente uncordiale between my chap and the Board, because the poor loves would surely be blamed for it. In despair I seized Morton Lee, the owner of a beautiful antique shop in the town, and told him my tale of woe. He pushed me into his car and raided his own cellar plus a large stock from the pub opposite him and drove me quickly back to the restaurant just before the bulk of the cast arrived. Honour and malt were satisfied and we settled down to unwind. I had a personal friend with me, Derek Ingram, who was the deputy editor of the *Daily Mail*. I took him as my guest to the party and had booked him a room at Woodend. We got back there about two o'clock. Larry heard us come in and asked us into his room for a nightcap. It was a fairly funny sight. Joan was in bed, Larry wore a dressing-gown and his old friends the Mills family who had been at the theatre were also there, having unexpectedly decided to stay the night. Mary and Hayley looked like an ad. for St. Tropez. Johnny's sole attire was one of Larry's short pyjama tops. We sat where we could and started letting our hair down. When actors get together their shop is probably the most amusing and scandalous of any profession. That night everything and everyone was sent up with reputations flying. Johnny and Larry egged each other on to tell intimate stories and give imitations of their friends to a captivated small audience. Tired but very exhilarated we said goodnight in the early hours and Larry told me how much he liked my friend. Little did he know that he had been entertaining one of the 'dreaded press' in, to say the least, rather strange circumstances.

Next morning I was longing to get to the theatre to see all the notices. Johnny gave me a lift. Mary and Hayley had rigged themselves out in some clothes borrowed from Joan and Johnny defiantly wore his evening shirt and trousers with a scarf round his neck. The papers were full of the event. Great space was given to the building, which got a lot of criticism: most of this was directed against the vastness of the stage although all of them welcomed a new theatre. Larry, too, was criticised for his choice of play; the general opinion being that it was too slight in plot and small wonder that it had not been performed for hundreds of years; although they were universal in their praise of individual performances and Larry's direction of it.

A mid-morning rehearsal had been called for the second play, *The Broken Heart*, which was to open the following Monday, and the company were already assembled in the theatre. Roger Furse, who had worked with Larry for years both in the theatre and on all his epic films, had done the decor for this curious, obscure play. It had been decided between the two of them to make the sets as elaborate and spectacular as possible. This involved part of the stage being sunk into an oblong trough resembling a small swimming bath. This had cost a fortune to achieve and was technically known as a podium but whenever Larry referred to the thing it was with heavy stress laid on the first syllable. For the next five days he slogged at rehearsals of *The Broken Heart* interspersed with those of *Uncle Vanya* and it became increasingly clear that he was close to exhaustion although he has been blessed by nature with an incredible constitution. But the superhuman task of choosing a company and repertoire, directing all three plays and acting in two of them was beginning to tell on him. He was finding great difficulty in memorising his lines for *The Heart*. At the weekend the Sunday notices for *The Chances* echoed the opinions expressed in the dailies except that they had even more

5a

5b

6a

6b

7a

7b

space in which to air them. The *Sunday Times* and the *Sunday Telegraph* were moderate in their criticism, but Kenneth Tynan in the *Observer* was very patronising. These, on top of the earlier notices, depressed Larry very much and did little to improve his temper and the rehearsal that day was punctuated with oaths. Relaxed and relieved after *The Broken Heart* first night was over, he invited me, Dorothy Tutin and some actors from the Aldwych to join him at the Curry Club. We were at the bar when a bucolic policeman entered, asking if anyone owned a Jaguar parked beside the restaurant. I went with him and recognised the car. Larry, thinking that I had at last overstepped the mark and done something frightful, came down to find what had happened. As if speaking to a moron, the constable demanded did he not know that he hadn't got a licence, it was an offence to drive without one and what did he propose to do about it? Larry blushed like a schoolboy and apologised profusely. I don't think he had much idea what the bobby was talking about because such details were always arranged for him by his secretary, but he promised 'not to do it again' and we returned to the restaurant. As we all left to go home he gave an oration in the street imitating exactly the young policeman's Sussex accent; as he drove off he put his head out of the window and with a lordly gesture said, 'Oi bid you farewell moy friends—you go back to Lunnon, moy place is here. Oi be a peripheral actor oi be!' and swept off.

Unfortunately the relaxed mood was not to last for long. I had arranged for all the papers to be delivered to Woodend the next morning. This Larry knew and sent a message for me to go up to his room. I dreaded it because the press had universally disliked not only the play itself but, also, Larry's performance had a lot of adverse criticism. Fearing m'lord's wrath I went tentatively into their room and handed him the papers. There was stony silence, broken only by the rustle of newspaper as each one was passed to Joan after he had read it. At last he looked up 'Well, Ginny darling, I'm *delighted* for Roger!' 'Roger?' I said. 'Yes. He's brought it off. It was worth *all* the trouble with the scenery.' I was shattered, it was the reaction I had least expected, I had even forgotten the critics had praised the décor because I was so upset for Larry. This unpredictability is one of the keynotes to his character which frequently misleads people. We had a cup of coffee after which he started, roundly and fundamentally, calling the press every epithet he could lay name to—his form of release.

In a determinedly gay mood he drove off to the theatre for a rehearsal of *Uncle Vanya*. There were no queues outside, and inside there was an air of gloom.

During the next few days there were feverish rehearsals for *Uncle Vanya*, the third and last play. Sean Kenny had designed the set which consisted of an enormous wooden false proscenium with a door and windows which became an exterior if lit from outside and the interior of a house if lit from behind. The stain that coloured it had to match with the colour of the wooden stage and the exact shade of this became an obsession with Larry. He had it changed about three times and I realised that he was applying his 'toothpaste' technique because he was desperately worried. The success of the first Chichester season depended now on *Uncle Vanya*; perhaps not only Chichester but also his future work at the National Theatre. Since the announcement of his appointment to this there had been an unsolicited campaign from certain members of the press involving the names of both Olivier and Peter Hall of the Royal Shakespeare

Company. Neither of them sought this partnership and Larry was too preoccupied to commit himself to any comment more than a mild 'I *do* wish they'd stop.' During that week the audiences were enthusiastic for *The Chances* but there were poor attendances for *The Broken Heart*. As we all knew the critical reaction to the play there was no anxiety about the Sunday press—at worst they could only be better. That shows just how wrong one can be. The *Observer* printed a notice in the shape of a letter from their critic Kenneth Tynan.

OPEN LETTER TO AN OPEN STAGER

Dear Sir Laurence,

We have now seen all but one of the three inaugural productions at Chichester, and I have to report a general feeling that all is not well with your dashing hexagonal playhouse. When you opened your season with *The Chances*, that flimsy Jacobean prank, one shrugged and wrote it off as a caprice; but when *The Broken Heart*, a far more challenging piece, likewise fails to kindle one's reflexes, it is time to stop shrugging and start worrying. Something has clearly gone wrong: but how? Who put the hex on the hexagon? Does the fault lie in the play, in the theatre, or in you, its artistic director?

First things first. The play is Ford's best tragedy, and history rightly says that Ford is not bunk. It also says (and here you may not agree) that on this occasion he composed a series of agonised tableaux rather than a continuously developing action. Nearly all the principal characters are mis-mated or sexually deprived. . . . To return, however, to reality: given a script so awkwardly split between nobility and banality, did you find a production style that might weld it together? I think not. You went all out for

67

anonymous rhetoric, 'fuyant le naturel'—as a French critic once put it—'sans trouver la grandeur'. A lot of vocal brandishing took place in a vacuum ... When in doubt about the precise emotion behind a speech, have it delivered in tones of ungovernable rage: was this, as I suspected, your watchword? ... And your own performance as Miss Harris's enforced husband? Surely Bassanes is a stupid, self-deluding dotard at whose ridiculous jealousy we are supposed to laugh until, in the course of time it becomes pathetic. You played him from the first as a sombre old victim bound for the slaughter, too noble and too tragic ever to be funny. Ford's tragedy was thus robbed of its essential comedy. Most remarkable of all you were indistinct: one lost more than half of what you said. And here begins my sad indictment of the peninsular Chichester stage ... the least desirable seats in the Globe Theatre—those occupied by the groundlings—were the ones nearest the stage. ... The picture-frame stage was invented in the seventeenth century to give all the spectators the same sight-lines and the same viewpoint; but it encouraged expensive décor, and in the last 50 years we have been urged to revive the projecting stage, ostensibly for artistic reasons but actually because it cuts scenic costs to a minimum. Chichester is a product of our gullibility: instead of letting the whole audience see the actors' faces (however distantly), we now prefer to bring them closer to the actors' backs. The Chichester stage is so vast that even the proximity argument falls down: an actor on the opposite side of the apron is farther away from one's front row seat than he would be from the twelfth row of a proscenium theatre—where in any case he would not deliver a crucial speech with his rear turned towards one's face. The more or less straight-edged stage (preferably stripped of the

68

proscenium framing) remains the most cunning and intimate method yet devised for transmitting plays to play-
goers: and it was on stages like this that you spent a
quarter of a century polishing your technique. Alas, at
Chichester your silky throwaway lines flicked at the
audience like leg-glances by Ranjitsinjhi, are literally
thrown away: they go for nothing and die unheard. In a
small theatre, where sound and sight present no problems,
the promontory stage is perfectly viable. In a large theatre
like Chichester's it simply does not work, above all if the
plays one is performing depend for their effect on verbal
nuance. You might point out to the National Theatre
Committee that, by recommending a stuck-out stage for
the main playhouse and proscenium for its junior partner,
they have got things exactly the wrong way round.

Tomorrow *Uncle Vanya* opens. Within a fortnight you
will have directed three plays and appeared in two leading
parts. It is too much. Do you recall the triumvirate, made
up of John Burrell, Ralph Richardson and yourself, that
ruled the Old Vic in those miraculous seasons between
1944 and 1946? Why not recruit a similar team to run the
National Theatre—a joint directorship consisting of yourself, Peter Brook and Anthony Quayle? I don't wish to be
dogmatic; I am merely dropping names, and hints.

The same Sunday morning scene as the previous week,
with Larry and Joan in bed, but a very different reaction.
Larry was genuinely hurt and upset, justifiably, by Tynan's
attack; not for himself but for the team who had worked
indefatigably to try and make Chichester a success. For the
very first time I saw his rage and anger, which lasted for ten
blistering minutes. Then he turned to Joan and said, 'Darling, in my most silky, throwaway tone I would suggest that

I employ Mr. Tynan at the National. In the time-honoured phrase "If you can't beat 'em, join 'em" and at least he would not be able to write notices about the theatre again.'

The following night was the opening of *Vanya*. The critics came into my office at the accustomed time and across the park came the familiar peacock-accoutred figure of Kenneth Tynan. To my amazement and secret delight, the office emptied and all his colleagues with their drinks in their hands went out to meet him. As one man they lifted their glasses and broke into a chorus of spontaneous raspberries and boos. Undaunted, he bowed, acknowledging their reception, entered the office and graciously accepted a drink. In the face of his associates' vocally expressed opinion I think he showed enormous nerve—or enormous egotism. In the press room I make it a rule never to discuss the play or the players with them but on this particular night the critics were overt in their enjoyment of the evening and offered their congratulations. Leaving them to write their notices I rushed over to Larry's dressing-room to tell him the news. 'Oh God, I hope you're right!' was the reply. His prayer was answered: next morning the critics were lavish in their praise and the season was vindicated.

Many weeks before the season opened it had been planned that there should be a charity gala performance during Goodwood week in the presence of the Queen. The Duke of Norfolk, with whom she was to stay, was the Patron of the theatre. On the occasions when royalty attend a theatre in a formal capacity the rules of etiquette and behaviour are made easy and simple for the hosts and their guests by the Palace liaison staff. A timetable is drawn up and a list of guests to be presented is exchanged so that everyone knows exactly what the procedure should be. Quite understandably Chichester lost its head over its first royal visit: the local press over-publicised it, the townspeople looked upon it as a Roman holiday and it became a dreaded nightmare to the theatre people who were long-accustomed to such occasions. The play chosen was *Uncle Vanya* and there were many fights among the hostesses of West Sussex as to which of them had procured seats nearest to the royal party—the fact that the position of these seats had not been disclosed did not deter their snobbish boasting. Plain-clothes police wandered around the park with pre-natal expressions for days before the event, culminating in the original idea that a wired fence should be erected round the edge of the theatre, the restaurant and the offices to hold back the expected crowds! The cathedral choir had prepared a version of the anthem to sing on Her Majesty's arrival in the auditorium. At the very last moment the Founder decided that instead of the dark blue plush that was used throughout for the seating, the royal party's seats would look better if they were covered in red velvet, and various members of the wardrobe department were hastily summoned from the Unicorn to carry out this task. It had been indicated via the Palace that the Queen and Prince Philip would like to meet the whole company after the show and the Committee should be presented during the interval. It poured with rain the entire day but the sun suddenly came out in the early evening. 'Founder's Weather' we muttered gladly and went down to the theatre. The small gathering of spectators looked pretty funny behind their hastily erected barricades and the entire West Sussex police force appeared to be on duty. The two official reporters and three photographers agreed by the Palace on the rota system arrived in my office. One of these, who had come from London by train, was wearing a rather shabby mackintosh, the others looked immaculate in evening dress. Suddenly there was a roar from the waiting crowd down by the

71

restaurant—we all looked at our watches which clearly told us that there was another ten minutes before the expected arrival. But the cheers increased and in horror we dashed over to the theatre. It was all too true, for once the royal party was ahead of time. It later transpired that the Duke of Norfolk's watch was fast and they were early in consequence. From then on everything was a little chaotic: the photographer hadn't had time to remove his offending mackintosh and was promptly grabbed by the over-enthusiastic police and frog-marched away to piteous cries of 'I'm an accredited man —you're taking my livelihood away! I'll have you put on a charge for this!'; quite a number of the audience were still drinking at the bar and had to be hustled ignominiously to their seats; and the guard of honour representing The Order of St. John and the British Red Cross Society were quickly called to stiff attention. They were inspected by Her Majesty in the foyer and certain presentations were made before the royal party entered the auditorium. Unfortunately, in the general confusion, no one had alerted the waiting cathedral choir who were to burst into song immediately the Queen arrived at her seat. Likewise the audience showed a small amount of uncertainty as to whether they should be seated or standing. There were a few seconds hesitation, some shuffling, the anthem started—and, with a sigh of relief from me, so had the evening.

Back in my office I tried to smooth down the ruffled photographer and promised that he could come into the theatre and get some exclusive shots of the Queen and the Duke meeting the company. A memo and chart had been circulated to all of us with the exact positioning of each person, grouped in a large half-horseshoe round the stage. It had been decided by Larry that Dame Sybil should take the Queen to her dressing-room and that he would entertain the

Duke in his. At the end of the performance I took the three photographers into the auditorium and stood in my place. Larry entered behind the Queen, accompanied by Prince Philip and Sybil Thorndike. He escorted Her Majesty, introducing her to each individual until he came to John Neville and had a 'stage dry', he simply could not remember the name, not only of one of his friends but also the god-father of his son! John himself came to the rescue and laughingly helped him out. Looking round at the empty theatre I spotted the Evershed-Martin family sitting in the second row and idly wondered why they were there as this part of the proceedings was for the professionals.

After the strain of the evening we went over to the restaurant for some food. Larry got into conversation with Mr. Evershed-Martin who asked if he had any plans for the following season. He replied that he had some unformulated plans but he had decided definitely to keep *Uncle Vanya* in the repertoire for the next year (it had only been seen at twenty-odd performances in the current programme). He was astonished to get the reply 'Over my dead body!' Roused with indignation that his artistic direction was being challenged he retaliated by again stressing that the planning and artistic policy would remain his responsibility and inferred that he suspected that the Company seemed to be working for the Founder's benefit. (In a different context he was to be proved correct. Five years later, fittingly, he was awarded the O.B.E.) This was greeted by a flood of tears from Mrs. Evershed-Martin who said that he, Larry, had ruined the most wonderful evening of their lives. They quickly left the restaurant, followed by Larry with immediate apologies. He knew that it was an unforgivable thing to have said, even in anger, and he was deeply sorry; he brooded on it for days and relations were never the same.

For fund-raising a ship, the *Windsor Castle*, anchored in Southampton, had been taken over for a night. Larry asked me if I would accompany him as he did not want Joan to be tired: she was by now five months pregnant. We arranged that we would drive over to Brighton, change there and leisurely make our way to Southampton. It was the first time I had seen the house completely finished and it looked lovely. We had a drink in the pale lilac drawing-room and wandered into the adjoining room which was Larry's study where he showed me his fascinating musée of theatrical souvenirs from the past and a number of Oscars and International awards that had been presented to him over the years. His comment was 'I suppose I was pretty grudging over accepting them but I don't think actors should be given *prizes*, although I'm sure it's all very flattering.' We had dinner and went upstairs to change. I had brought three different dresses with me and Larry insisted on a tiny 'costume parade' to decide which he preferred. This was followed with a further discussion on what jewellery should be worn. I was secretly very amused by this extraordinary attention to detail which is second nature to him. He himself can get totally involved in his own choice of tie! When I had passed muster we set off. We hadn't gone very far before he asked me if I had heard from Vivien recently, saying that although he was ideally happy in his present marriage he still had desperate regrets and conscience about her. He told me that the first ten years of their married life were the happiest he had ever known but he had been miserable for a long time before they were eventually divorced. He added that he had similar feelings when he parted from his first wife and that he could never endure another divorce. 'I can never rid myself of my appalling guilt conscience, not just over the inevitable split but over everything.' He referred back again to his early childhood and his adored mother. I think Joan, who is so calm and maternal, has quite unconsciously become a mother-symbol to him. He told me, with pride, that 'Joanie doesn't want a baby—she wants babies.' I knew what he meant. After years of fighting to achieve ephemeral ambitions he now longed for a tangible domestic background with continuity. I asked him if he believed in God and his answer was 'No, I wish I could.' I told him I did in a completely unorthodox way and pressed him to agree with me that there must be some sort of over-all concept that gave us belief. His reply was that he thought the early years when he used to listen to his father preaching sermons, and his church upbringing, had perhaps contributed to making him an unbeliever, but that the pomp and panoply of the Church had left a lasting impression on him and on his work. It's odd, I thought, he's denying this too vehemently and I don't believe it's true. From religion we passed on to politics: here again he had no strong views. He told me he had been brought up a Tory but had leanings towards Socialism for the principles without much confidence in the practice. We both agreed on this and he came to the conclusion that he was a-religious and a-political. Chatting idly, I asked him if he had any hobbies; did he read much? The answer was 'Plays, Ginny, and more plays.' He enjoyed concerts, which he seldom went to, the theatre, mainly as part of his work, and various serials on T.V. as relaxation. Holidays he dislikes, chiefly because he rarely has sufficient time to enjoy them. I noted this with interest because I had found that he had very little patience with anyone round him who was away on hols for more than a few days, and also remembered he had scant sympathy with illness. I speculated whether this stemmed from his acute anxiety caused by Vivien's various indispositions or the natural reactions of a healthy man towards disease. All the years I had known him he had practically never been ill or missed a performance apart from minor injuries incurred by over-zealous jumps or falls in the course of his work. When any of these accidents took place he would go into incredible detail with his doctor in order to find the exact medical name of his complaint: for instance, when he slipped a cartilage in *Richard III* he said that he had damaged the anterior medial horn of the miniscus of his right leg, and a sore throat would become an acute attack of the laringeal chords of the pharynx. He was delighted when I swopped 'acute coryza'—common cold—with him. I told him the story of a certain actor who was contemplating having a sex operation. Larry's reaction was 'Oh the poor, *silly* darling, he's left it too late—he's going to become a woman and start having the change of life!'

As we approached the docks his usual horror came over him at the prospect of having to live up to his own legend. He quietly asked me if I had got enough money on me to pay for the various games and lotteries that we would have to indulge in, and slipped me a couple of pounds for luck. Facing the battery of televsion cameras at the head of the gangway we made for the self-operated lift. 'Would you care for lingerie or the pet's department, modom?' as he pressed one of the buttons. 'God, you might just as well be in a bloody hotel!' We stepped out on A deck and immediately he became the professional Entertainer. A few hours later, and quite a few pounds lighter, we set off for Brighton. His relief at having got it over nearly caused our end because he did not notice we were still in the dockyard and it is always a good idea to give way to an oncoming train —even on a siding. 'Sorry, darling, I wasn't expecting that.' Well, what could one reply except a weak 'I didn't see it either,' a hollow lie!

We were both ravenous when we got back and Larry made some scrambled eggs and told me to sleep late the following day and buzz when I woke up. This was always my Waterloo. There is a complicated system of communication which embraces the four floors and the intermediary half landings, consisting of terrifying lights that flash on and off accompanied by alarming buzzing noises. These are allied with a splendid service lift that does the same thing. There are notices warning guests of the horrors that may befall them if they open or close the door at the wrong moment or likewise push the wrong bell. Being totally unmechanical, these labour-saving devices put the fear of God into me, particularly when I can clearly hear Larry saying on the intercom in the tone one would adopt to an idiot child, 'Darling, all you have to do is press it.' A few evenings later the 'bells' turned the table on him. He had been entertaining some friends in the restaurant some hundred yards away from the theatre and was slightly late back in the interval. His own recorded reassuring words came booming out 'Ladies and gentlemen, there are three minutes left, please take your seats.' He took to his heels and ran towards the theatre shouting 'Oh, for God's sake shut up you silly sod!'

After all the plays had been launched Eric and Mary Bessborough invited the company to an informal barbecue. The gardens of their home are vast and there is a huge superheated swimming pool. It was gorgeous and hot during the day but in the afternoon the heavens opened, old Thor had a good go, and the temperature dropped to near freezing. Undaunted, a cold buffet was swiftly assembled indoors; the company arrived with bikinis under arms and, helped by lashings of drink, the party got under way. Around midnight the cast became divided: led by Rosemary Harris a number disported 'tout nus' in the tepid water while the rest

77

huddled round a log fire in the Roman room leading from the pool. Insidiously a nasty smell pervaded it which emanated from Joan Greenwood's handbag. As it smouldered she snatched it and gurgled 'How deleecious! I've always adored roast crocodile!'

Suddenly we realised that the season was coming to an end. The last night was *Uncle Vanya* and at the finish of the play the audience applauded for ten solid minutes. Afterwards a champagne party was given for us by the Board in the foyer. Leslie Evershed-Martin inaugurated a strange custom. He had bought a large silver loving-cup which was filled with champagne and solemnly handed round to everyone to drink from. When it came to Larry's turn he tentatively wiped it with a napkin, toasted the Founder, looked round and said 'There's no one here with the surname Borgia, is there?'

The first Chichester season was over with surprisingly little blood drawn.

3

Plans for 'The National'

LARRY had agreed to appear in a comedy called *Semi-Detached* in the autumn. This was a new play by an unknown playwright, David Turner, and at the first reading everyone fell about with laughter. The action was set in the Midlands, Turner's part of the world, and it was very noticeable at the reading that Larry was using a heavy Birmingham accent. He had spent hours listening to recordings and talking to Midlanders in order to perfect it. The rest of the small cast, which included Mona Washbourne, Eileen Atkins and Patsy Rowlands, made little attempt at authenticity but seemed easier to understand and we thought Larry would tone it down when he got going. But as rehearsals progressed it became obvious that he was aiming at a totally convincing Birmingham wide-boy. In fact, he went there to buy his suits from a small gent's outfitters who specialised in cheap off-the-peg clothes and to break them down insisted on wearing them during the day for the remainder of the rehearsals. The play was due to open in Edinburgh and we travelled up over the weekend. I went to Larry's room at the dress rehearsal and had a shock. He was wearing not one but two wigs: the first was like a shiny bald egg and the second had a little hair plastered on it; the effect was completed by a nasty drooping moustache. He looked revolting. I'm afraid I told him so. He was very hurt and said that he had modelled himself on his father-in-law. Maybe, but that didn't make him any the more attractive.

The good citizens of Edinburgh were shocked by the play —heaven knows why. It was a satire with witty dialogue and the Lord Chamberlain's blessing but the reception was only mildly enthusiastic. I heard a member of the audience whisper in thrilled tones 'May, it was vairy salaycious, eh?' It was scheduled to open at the Saville Theatre within a few weeks and I had persuaded the London Committee of the Festival Theatre to buy the pre-view for a fund-raising scheme. At noon on the appointed day a veritable pea-souper fog came down and anxious telephone calls were exchanged regarding the advisability of cancelling it. It was decided this would be impossible and I set off for the theatre. Inside it seemed almost as thick as it was outside. A trickling of audience, muffled up to their eyebrows, wandered in looking as if they were on their way to a wake rather than a jolly funny play. Although there were not many of them, they coughed and spluttered throughout the evening, too uncomfortable to pay any heed to the stage. It was disaster. I went round afterwards and tried to cheer Larry up but it didn't do much good and I'm sure it had a bad effect on the following night because the humour and the acting seemed to be forced. The notices were mixed and on the whole lukewarm. It ran for a number of weeks quite successfully but Larry was utterly miserable playing the part. Whenever I went round to his dressing-room he was always praying for it to come off. It was the time of the school holidays and parents used to bring their young children to see the great Olivier happily imagining their offspring would see a memorable performance. They did, but perhaps not the kind they had in mind. The public seldom know the subject of a play and Larry's reputation at the time was synonymous with Shakespeare and the classics. They also did not realise that remarks made during a performance can be heard on the stage—particularly at a half full matinée—and he was frequently disturbed to learn that he was offending the grown-ups and upsetting the children. So much did this affect him that it brought on an attack of gout that forced him to be away for a few performances. Possibly the birth of his first daughter in January, with whom he fell instantly and totally in love, was a contributory factor as he takes himself deadly seriously as a parent and I think it depressed him that the child audiences did not respond to him as a father figure. I have never known any actor to be as happy as he was when the last two weeks were announced; at the same time he blamed himself for the play's failure. I'm sure this wasn't true but in some odd way the public refused to accept the character he portrayed and maybe it would have succeeded with a more conventional comedian in the role.

Immediately he started working on the plans for the next Chichester season. He had selected the plays which were to be Shaw's *Saint Joan*, *The Workhouse Donkey*, a new play by John Arden and—most certainly—*Uncle Vanya*. At the same time he was deeply occupied with National Theatre meetings and appointments of his personnel. It was decided that there would be a triumvirate of directors consisting of Larry at the head with John Dexter and William Gaskill, both of whom had done admirable work at the Royal Court, working under him. True to his word at Chichester, he approached Kenneth Tynan to join the organisation and he accepted. During the run of *Semi-Detached* it had been agreed that I too should become part of it. Possibly the biggest thrill of my life was putting out the first official announcement of these appointments to the press. For more than a hundred years the idea of a National theatre in England had been mooted and there was a curious feeling of permanence mixed with unreality when I wrote the words 'the National Theatre' for the first time and knew that this was a piece of theatrical history. I was asked to meet Stephen Arlen—on loan from Sadlers Wells for a year to help launch the National—at Kenneth Tynan's flat where Larry would join us. I hadn't seen Ken since Chichester last year and had never known him intimately. The appointment was for three o'clock and I was the first to arrive at his apartment in Mount Street. A woman opened the door and told me Mr. Tynan was still in bed. I was shown into a big sitting-room and asked to wait. I sat down with the slightly apprehensive feeling one has in a strange place and looked round me. On the back wall, covering the entire space, was an enormous blown-up photograph of Hieronymus Bosch's multi-sexual orgy. I noted it with amusement and wondered if it was designed as a shock tactic for visitors or as a memo for himself. Larry and Stephen arrived together and Ken came gaily bounding into the room with apologies. This meeting was to decide on the various titles: Larry's was simply the Director; with Stephen as Administrative Director and the two 'boys', Bill and John, as Associate Directors. This left Ken's splendid nomenclature. He had a strong idea of his own which derived from the European theatre. He said he would like to be known as the 'dramaturg', which Roget's Thesaurus lists under the heading of *Imitation* as: mime, pantomime, sign language, gesticulation; and Chamber's Dictionary succinctly says: a playwright. (Through French from Greek *dramatourgia*, *dramatourgos*, Playwright—*drama* and *ergon*, A Work.) After some discussion the conclusion was reached that perhaps the English theatre was not quite ready for this unaccustomed word and the more comprehensible title

'Literary Manager' was agreed on. I was sitting silent while all this chat was going on and thinking how oddly important the choice of silly titles was to men. Is this why war appeals to them so much? Lovely uniforms; lovely ranks; putting them automatically above the others? All these thoughts were chasing through my mind until I realised that the same question was going to be asked me in a moment. 'Projector and Protector?' Well, why not—it would sum up the job I did, but I didn't think I would get away with it. My musing was abruptly interrupted by Larry who said, 'Ginny, I suppose you'll be our P.R.O.?' I suddenly heard myself replying 'If it means "professional" I bloody well should be, otherwise I'm not fit for the job, and if it means the wartime phrase "Public Relations Officer" then I'm the wrong sex.' There was a tiny pause before I was asked what I would like to be called. 'Press Representative', I replied and it was accepted without argument.

In the following weeks before rehearsals began for the second Chichester season, Larry was constantly in the company of John Dexter and William Gaskill who he always referred to as his 'boys', although they were both approaching forty. He was nearly twenty years older and, for a number of months, he seemed to have an almost frenetic desire to be 'with it' which showed in his vocabulary and in some fairly fearsome clothes he bought. The 'boys' in turn started to call him 'Dad', whether in affection or mockery was difficult then to judge. Dexter was to direct *Saint Joan*, the first play at Chichester. In order to concentrate as much as possible on the National Larry was only appearing in *Uncle Vanya*. I had one of my more idiotic publicity ideas: the company and everyone connected with it from Chichester should be photographed in one of those nasty groups with an illustrated 'Key' for identification. It took many days' careful planning

83

to ensure that everybody could be present and a special coach was laid on to bring the staff from Chichester. The day arrived and the group, totalling over a hundred people, were being assembled into some sort of shape when Joan Plowright told me privately that Larry would not be able to make it as he had to attend a meeting! Oh splendid, I thought, Hamlet without the Prince. However I went over to Angus McBean who was taking the picture and told him the problem. 'A man!' cried Angus, 'Any man will do and I will superimpose Larry's head on afterwards.' Easy, except there wasn't one until Joan remembered the chauffeur who was sitting outside in the car. He was dragged in, his cap pulled off him and he was pushed in the centre. Unfortunately he had a great bull neck and enormous shoulders and when the photograph with the montage was finished it was palpably obvious that the camera *could* lie. I gave it to the *Daily Mail* who ran a story headed 'Spot the deliberate mistake'. It was being rumoured in Fleet Street that the Chichester Company were to be the nucleus of the first National Theatre Company which, though not known then by the actors, was to prove true.

While the London rehearsals were in progress I was ceremoniously introduced to the small collection of people who comprised the staff of the National. They were headed by Kenneth Rae, the Secretary to the Board, who had been advocating and working for the formation of it for nearly twenty years. He is a tall, distinguished, grey-haired man with a wonderful sense of humour—very necessary—who, to my joy, I remembered I had met a few years back. The offices were situated in Goodwin's Court leading off St. Martin's Lane where Nell Gwynne once lived. They were as charming and friendly as the occupants themselves. Unfortunately everyone was shortly to move to the other side of the river where temporary offices were being erected on an old bombed alley. I was taken to see them by Kenneth. We had to pick our way over a mess of rubble, old iron bedsteads, broken bottles and suchlike filth to a row of very unimpressive huts which ran the length of the little alley. 'My God!' I said to Kenneth, 'we're really squandering the taxpayer's money!' He replied that they were third-hand workmen's site huts and that is exactly what they looked and smelled like. He explained they would not be in use for longer than four years at the very outside. Unfortunately they are still standing —just—as I am writing this and quite likely to be there for another four or five years, if they don't fall down from decay.

A few weeks before the season started we all moved to Chichester. Larry rented a house because there were now two babies and two nannies and they needed more rooms than Woodend could manage. Everybody looked forward with keen anticipation to Joan Plowright's interpretation of *Saint Joan*. After her performance in *Roots* it seemed as if Shaw must have had her in mind when he wrote the play; it was such perfect casting. I attended one of the early run-throughs, without costumes or scenery, and spent most of the afternoon with a sodden handkerchief and my face streaked with mascara. As always after rehearsals notes are given by the producer (in this case John Dexter) and they were continued in private at the Oliviers' house that evening. Next day, and thereafter, an emasculated note crept into her performance and the emotion was toned down which caused the critics to complain that she lacked heart. I have always suspected that the original conception was inspired by Larry and ironed out by John. This was the first instance of the influence the younger Royal Court school-trained executives of the organisation exerted over Larry, rightly or wrongly. Although he has a forward-thinking and searching mind he is inclined to be led and influenced by people round him, not always for the better. This is partly his fear of approaching age and being called old-hat.

Just after the season had opened David telephoned me from London where he was engaged on West End productions and said he would particularly like me to spend a couple of days in town with him in the middle of the week. This I agreed to do and arranged to go into the National offices for a meeting while I was up there. When I got to London David told me that we were going to get married the following morning. I had changed my name by deed poll and we had been living together for so many years that it had slipped my notice that we were not legally married, although his divorce had been granted some two years back. In one way it is simpler to get a divorce than it is to get married when everyone believes that you are already; it sort of seems embarrassing. However, he had arranged it all and there it was. I rang Larry and explained why I couldn't attend the next day's meeting and he was amused and delighted; I begged him to keep silent and make excuses for my absence which he promised to do. Later that evening Ken Tynan, who had heard I would not be present the following day, suggested that I should defer my personal appointment to a later date in view of the points to be discussed at the meeting. I decided to tell him the true reason. Slightly taken aback, his reaction was typical: 'I suppose you sh-should be there—how very sweet and old-fashioned.'

During this Chichester season there was only one 'must' for the company to attend. This was a race meeting at Fontwell Park which had been organised for the Building Fund. It was the first sponsored meeting of its kind and it had been specially fitted into the Racing Calendar. I don't think any of the actors had much idea about racing but they understood they had to be present. Fontwell is a small course, much more intimate and friendly than either Sandown, Kempton or its neighbour, Goodwood. For this meeting all the tents were run by the sponsors and the whole atmosphere was like a family party. Rehearsals were broken at midday and the actors started to arrive. I spotted a slightly distracted Michael Redgrave, obviously looking for a familiar face. He greeted me with relief and said he thought he ought to back a horse and 'how was it done?' I told him to follow me to the tote. On the way he confessed he had never been to a race meeting in his life before and only had £2 on him. When I conducted him to the four shilling booth he joined the queue for the pound tickets; across the barriers I shouted that he was in the wrong place. Nothing daunted he placed his all on a complete outsider and we went up to the stands to watch the race. With beginner's luck his choice romped home and he was overcome with excitement and suggested having a drink to celebrate. I gently reminded him that he had to collect his winnings to buy me one. He looked amazed when he was handed a fistful of notes and, very wisely, spent the rest of the afternoon wandering about. When Larry and Joan arrived they were immediately given some lunch in one of the tents and Larry, also a non-gambler, asked how he could place a bet. Jim Battersby assured him it was simple: there was a telephone in the tent and he could put his bet on with one of the London firms. Fascinated by this he had a look at the card and saw there was a horse called Dark Venetian. He thought for a moment and said, 'Sired by Black Tarquin— that's my son's name and that dreaded part Othello is, God knows, BLACK in its nastiest sense, so I'll try it.' He rang the bookie and boldly announced he would like £20 on the horse. I suppose I should have known better and followed suit. Needless to say the damned thing won and it was fairly funny a little later to see the two highly-paid theatrical knights dancing about and mutually congratulating each other on their winnings like excited schoolboys. For many months prior to the meeting there had been a coast to coast raffle, the prize being a racehorse. The winner could either keep the horse or have the equivalent in money—in this case £1,000. It was a three-year-old and had already won two races. It was due to run this afternoon with a jolly good jockey on it, in the last and highest sponsored race. With local photographers and television cameras lined up Larry was to present the cup at the finish of the race. Flushed with confidence and triumph at having won, and feeling every inch a veteran race-goer, he walked into the paddock and patted the horse's nose with a proprietary air and gaily chatted to the jockey. He wished him luck and hoped he wouldn't 'fall off'. Fatal, of course. He did—at the very last tiny hurdle while leading by lengths. Larry's insatiable guilt conscience came to the fore and he blamed himself for talking to the jockey!

In the theatre rumours were buzzing about the first actors to be signed for the National. Interviews were constantly held in Larry's little dressing-room and gossip multiplied regarding the salaries being offered and accepted. The 'opening date' varied from person to person and the 'opening play' covered anything from *Mourning Becomes Electra* to *Charley's Aunt*. Eventually I bearded Larry and said I wanted a chat. I went back to the rented house with him and he told me the plans. He said that instead of taking over the theatre in September as visualised, the National was going to lease it as soon as the current play, *Measure for Measure*, ended its run. This meant that the envisaged alterations to the auditorium, the stage and back-stage could begin earlier than had been anticipated, thereby making it possible to present the first production in mid-autumn. After a good deal of discussion it was decided to hold a press conference up in London to announce the plans for the National. This was the first of many and was remarkable for only three things: it was discovered that Laurence Olivier was superb at making extempore speeches and even better at answering loaded questions; that it was a very bad idea to sit the press in serried rows as if they were back at school; and, lastly, Kenneth Tynan coined a phrase that was to become the slogan of the N.T. and the ambiguous answer to hundreds of enquiries as to future plans and policy. This was 'We aim to present a spectrum of world drama.'

Privately I discovered that Viscount Chandos, the Chairman, was a very understanding gentleman. After the conference I had the audacity to ask him if he would be an angel and wait for ten or fifteen minutes because there were a number of press photographers who wanted to take a picture of him and Larry together. (Larry was still being chatted up by the journalists.) His courteous reply was: 'Certainly Mrs. Fairweather, provided you can rustle up a large gin and tonic I am prepared to wait until the knight is out.'

4

The First National Theatre

WHEN the 1963 Chichester Season closed all of the 'National-
ists' had a holiday, including even Larry. I moved into the
office in the middle of September. It was pretty much as I
had seen it in June. The walls were painted a rich dun colour
and a disgusting shade of blue joined it halfway. I sought
permission to buy my own material and have it re-decorated.
This was granted and I chose white, forest green and yellow
to give an illusion of fresh air and space, but I could never
stop the wild cats fornicating under the creaking floorboards.
The offices are sandwiched between a block of six-storey
council flats on one side and on the other a high bombed
wall, where houses once stood, with a row of buildings over-
looking them. The ceilings are low and the windows tiny,
excluding what little daylight might have been able to filter
through. At the extreme end there is a large, cold rehearsal
room and, looking up the long corridor as through a tele-
scope, there are a myriad of tiny offices leading off either
side of the narrow passage ending in 'the Board Room', with
a final little honeycomb housing the accountants. There is a
tank outside the rehearsal room where oil for the heating is

delivered. This is a great joke. Although on regular contract the suppliers are erratic except for one certainty: if the weather turns cold they fail to turn up. On the other hand, due to the primitive installation, it is utterly impossible to cool the place in the summer because the hot pipes are overhead and run the entire length of the building and cannot be turned off although the sole need is to heat four handbasins at the lower end. To sum up—cold in winter, hot in summer, impossible to locate and totally unhealthy. They are situated ten minutes walk away from the Old Vic. This is always a hazardous trip: one has to push through a horde of multi-racial children hellbent on torment, walk past hundreds of incontinent pigeons nesting on the Waterloo archways, try to avoid the masses of methylated spirit drinkers fighting and swearing in dear Emma Cons commemorative garden in front of the theatre before reaching one's objective. Bringing the masses to culture? Maybe, but all very squalid. Anyway the pioneering spirit was uppermost again but this time in real earnest. Chichester with its originality, its voluntary start and its amateur background was one thing but the National was completely different. This time the eyes of the world were on us, with a section of the public prejudiced against us and we had to prove our worth.

The choice for the inaugural production was *Hamlet* with Peter O'Toole as the Prince and Sean Kenny as designer. Larry himself was to direct it. Owing to film commitments Peter was a guest artist and could only appear for a short time, which amounted in fact to twenty-seven performances. Because of the policy to create a repertoire presenting different plays at each performance there were three first nights in the first four weeks: *Hamlet*, followed by *Saint Joan* and *Uncle Vanya*—both from Chichester. Every possible inch of spare space, of which there was little, was in use. To further complicate things the next production, *The Recruiting Officer* was also under way. Some of the time schedules for the actors read like a Kafka nightmare. Many were rehearsing in three plays at the same time. Primary importance was given, very naturally, to *Hamlet*. Sean Kenny's set was deceptively simple in design. It consisted of a huge tiered half circle of solid construction mounted on a revolve. From the outset of it being assembled on the stage it became evident that the underworld technicians below stage level were going to have a little trouble. During the pre-opening dress rehearsals the revolve developed a hideous personality of its own and was soon nicknamed the 'Revolt'. The set and the production had been envisaged together to move fluidly and carry the action forward as the play was to be performed in its entirety, lasting four and a half hours. Somehow the damned thing always stuck at some point, never in the same place twice! Long before the opening night a 'book' was made on which scene it would stick.

How can one capture the curious feelings of terrified excitement everyone had just before the first night loomed? It isn't possible. Starting the National was making theatre history, but with a sense of inadequacy for the occasion—perhaps that is how all history is made. For my own part all I did was to develop migraine that lasted for three solid weeks.

The dreaded night came and departed and next morning the dreaded press reports were infinitely kinder than they might have been. With scant time for rehearsals, masses of unexpected problems to be smoothed out, and the fact that the company were comparatively unknown to each other, the production was uneven both in acting and direction but the revolve behaved impeccably at every turn. Unfortunately its notices must have gone to its well-oiled head because the following day it refused to work properly after the interval.

The 'book' for the iron horse Revolt increased its adherents. Now the hazards were (a) will the curtain go up? (b) when will it stick? and (c) will the show go on? The odds were heavily against the first and the last and they lengthened in a sporting way for the middle. Each performance was feared by the cast and the poor darling technicians who tended and nursed the damn thing hourly were convinced that some horrible gremlin had crept into their midst. *Saint Joan* joined the repertoire in the second week and *Uncle Vanya* in the fifth. These additional plays meant that Revolt had to be dismantled and re-assembled when *Hamlet* was being played. After four free nights *Hamlet* was given again. Revolt decided to conk out completely towards the end of the play. Luckily it did not greatly matter that night but it became something of grave concern for the following matinée. The loyal backstage staff worked ceaselessly throughout the night but the beastly thing refused to budge. Early the next morning an emergency meeting was called, headed by Larry, Stephen Arlen—himself an ex-stage director with expert knowledge—and the cast. Orders had been given to me to keep it from the press if possible and the three of us proceeded from the offices to the theatre. Stephen asked me if I would care to look at 'it' and we went down into the bowels of the stage. There we found seven or eight unshaven, haggard gentlemen on their hands and knees staring into a very small space which contained the actual workings of this mammoth structure. Everything had been tried by our own staff and the installers had been called in, but all to no avail. I went up to the stage and found a strange sight. Revolt was stationary and the cast were re-rehearsing their exits and entrances in groups of twos and threes. This was necessary because so much of the action took place on the set itself. Larry was standing leaning against one of the proscenium

93

arches watching and giving advice; after a few minutes of this he suddenly called the stage manager and demanded to know if everyone of the cast was present. Yes, came the reply. 'Are you quite sure *everyone*, even the non-speakers?' The ominous voice quailed the poor stage manager but she stuck her ground. 'Oh damn and blast!' he moaned, 'Why couldn't someone have had a cold? I would give anything to be with you lot this afternoon, even walking on.' He meant it: his company were in a tight spot and he wanted to help if he could. He talked to the packed audience before the curtain went up and gently explained what had happened; he did not make any overt apologies, but on a wry note suggested they could have their money back if they had not enjoyed his production. Nobody took advantage of this offer and it was a remarkable performance with the actors as nervous as on the first night. Oddly enough the vagaries of Revolt did not get into the press, probably because there were numerous other rumours running around Fleet Street and the West End about the National!

The following year, 1964, was the Quatercentenary of Shakespeare's birth and there were many, many discussions about the play to be given to mark it. Although the National by intent did not perform many of his plays, the choice of the birthday presentation was fairly obvious. Othello was the only major Shakespearean tragic role that Larry had never played although he had appeared as Iago with Richardson as the Moor before the war. For years he had strenuously refused to attempt this most demanding of parts and now intense pressure was brought to bear on him to change his mind. He was wheedled and cajoled by the three 'boys'; Ken, quite rightly, thought it would be a huge box-office attraction, John dearly wanted to direct it, and Larry, in such an important production and both he (John) and Bill Gaskill wished to give Frank Finlay—who had been with the Royal Court for some time with great success—a bigger opportunity and cast him as Iago. In the face of all these arguments, with grave doubts and misgivings, Larry gave in. From then on until the play was due to open in the spring of 1964 he gave himself up to training physically and mentally for the part.

There were now three plays running concurrently in the repertoire and the next was to be *The Recruiting Officer*, an early eighteenth century satirical comedy. This was William Gaskill's first production for the National with that gorgeous comedienne Maggie Smith in the lead and Michael Redgrave's younger daughter, Lynn, playing a tiny part. Larry, too, was cast in a small role as the braggadocio Captain Brazen. This gave him wonderful scope to be outrageously funny. The rehearsal schedule for this, which was to become common practice, was six weeks with two dress rehearsal weekends, without an audience, prior to the opening date. The first weekend was attended by John Dexter, Kenneth Tynan and various staff connected with the production. Even with that small assembly Larry made them yell with laughter every time he appeared. Ken was sitting next to me and I was startled to hear him moaning to himself at their reaction. 'God, don't they see he's overdoing everything? It's awful and old-fashioned—he's not a real character, he's a real caricature!' At the end John came over to us. 'Well,' he asked Ken, 'what did you think of him?' 'Bloody dreadful!' was the succinct reply. They both made their way down to the edge of the stage and joined William Gaskill in giving notes, and gave their opinions that Larry was wildly overplaying and throwing the rest of the production out of gear. He took this criticism seriously and with great interest, although he seemed a little surprised, but he heeded it and toned his performance down and still managed to capture all the notices.

At Christmas time Larry decided to call a meeting of all the fathers in the company and give a children's party. This was organised for Christmas Eve before the Tuesday evening performance. Everyone, including Ivan Alderman—head of the wardrobe and the props department, weighed in to help and anyone connected with the organisation who owned a child was welcome to bring it. The old rehearsal room had been decked out with streamers and coloured lanterns and a massive decorated tree loaded with presents dominated one end. There were about fifty children, ranging from two to eleven years old, with a hundred anxious adults keeping things in some semblance of order. Before starting tea they had all been told Father Christmas was to visit them. Little did they know that he had not arrived down the chimney but was cursing and swearing in the Lilian Baylis room trying to get his mammoth beard to stick securely. With a fanfare he arrived up in the room. Never has any benevolent gentleman essaying this role looked so formidable. There was immediate silence from the children—I should think from sheer fright. A voice as from the netherworld issued from Larry's lips in a 'cosy reassuring' little welcoming speech. From silence there was instant pandemonium. Nearly fifty kids started to cry together, his own son leading the din. Far more terrified than the children, he tried desperately to put things right. He seized one of the nearest tots and carried her over to the tree and gave her a large doll—she clutched it to her tiny bosom and did her best to 'Ooh!' instead of 'Aah'. The grown-ups were torn between laughter and trying to calm the children. They hustled them up to the tree and the presents were quickly distributed and Larry made his exit. As he went, his son Richard turned to a very beautiful but alarmed little girl, put his arm round her shoulder and said, with a great show of false bravery, 'I'm not afraid, it's my Dada—I fink!' I went down to the dressing-room and found Larry in a hell of a state. He was utterly shattered at this unique reception to his performance and kept asking himself where he'd gone wrong! Luckily there was no John, Ken or Bill to tell him.

From the moment that he had finally agreed to play Othello, Larry went into vigorous training. He started to take intensive voice production classes to lower his register, and redoubled his sessions at the gymnasium. These were mainly concerned with weight-lifting to strengthen and broaden his lungs and breathing. He was fifty-seven years old and he had read that one of the earlier Othellos (Macready?) suffered with palpitations for forty-eight hours after playing it and knew that, although he was physically very strong, it would put great strain on his constitution. The National's first provincial tour was listed for the spring of '64 and *Othello* was to be one of the highlights before opening in London. Apart from his appearances in *Uncle Vanya* and *The Recruiting Officer*, plus rehearsals for *Othello*, he was greatly involved in the day-to-day running of the theatre and in formulating plans for Chichester. One day towards the end of January Joan telephoned from Brighton to say that he was not feeling too well and would stay in bed for a couple of days. Those two days lengthened into ten and alarm set in. Time was getting short for the out of town opening of *Othello* and it was imperative that he returned as soon as possible. His doctors were contacted but they appeared to be baffled. His temperature had a nasty habit of going up many degrees in the evening but was comparatively normal during the day. They were unable to diagnose the condition specifically, calling it generally a 'virus infection'. It was decided to omit the play from the repertoire for the first part of the tour and open it in Birmingham. I went down to Brighton while he was still in bed and he told me a story against himself. A few days earlier, when his temperature had remained normal for a number of hours, he had made up his mind to get some fresh sea air. Never one for taking the easy way in anything, this had to be done as a major exercise. He had imagined that his muscles had become flabby while lying in bed and when he got up for his 'ozone' he solemnly dressed himself in a track suit and set off at a spanking pace running along the front towards Black Rock. He had covered about a mile when his legs gave out and he realised that he was weak, winded and far from home. Reeling and swaying, he tried to attract the attention of passing motorists to no avail. In desperation he stopped two women who were walking in the direction of Royal Crescent and, sobbing for breath, begged them to see him home, explaining who he was. With outraged indignation one of them looked him up and down and replied, 'Don't talk nonsense—you should be ashamed of yourself to be in that condition at this hour of the morning!' Too far gone to argue, he sat at the edge of the road with tears streaming down his face until a friendly tradesman recognised him and took him in his van to the house where he was sent straight back to bed.

He recovered, with his usual ebullience, and came back to work with renewed vigour. During the time he had been absent John had re-directed much of the play. This did not become immediately apparent because of the urgency to rehearse the *Othello* scenes. Larry himself had spent his enforced absence working on his own part as it had been originally set. The new moves temporarily threw him out but there

98

was no time to spare for argument. Derek Salberg, the managing director of the Alexandra Theatre in Birmingham, was most helpful and co-operative. He arranged that the play that finished there on Saturday night should be got out as quickly as possible and our technicians would take over and set-up during that night to enable us to have two dress rehearsals on Sunday. The first was a 'technical' run through, followed by a full rehearsal in the evening. Ken had arrived during the day and we sat together in the stalls to watch. As the play progressed it became very clear that something was wrong. The opening scenes were taken at a conversational gabble and were quite impossible to comprehend. The conception of Iago as a contemporary soldier with a grudge is perfectly valid but it is essential to speak the words clearly in order to be able to understand the plot (which the character carries to a great extent). This, originally, Frank Finlay failed to do. The lack of balance became even more obvious in the duologues between Iago and Othello and some of the crowd scenes were a jumbled mess. Ken was busily making notes during the first half. At the interval the two of us went over to the pub for a drink. He was questioning the choice of John as director for this, his first attempt at a Shakespearean play, and said Larry should have produced it with John, adding that if it opened in its present state it would be disaster. I wholeheartedly agreed with him and we went back for the second half in harmony.

Apart from a few desultory notes, little was said to Larry that night. He was tired and exhausted and went to bed early. Ken and I sat up fairly late discussing the play and we both concluded that the best thing to happen would be if Larry took over the production before it came to London, even at this late stage. Ken's notes and script emendations were delivered to him with breakfast. His reaction was cautious. Although I am sure he agreed in principle, he did not want to throw Frank on his first night nor upset John; but he attended the morning rehearsal—although he had been released from it—and made a few important suggestions that were incorporated. In the afternoon he invited Frank into his dressing-room while he was making up—this operation took three and a half hours—and very gently went over the opening scenes with him. He wisely decided that the most important ones involving the two of them should be left until Frank had got over his first night nerves. God only knows what he suffered with his own nerves on that night, which he had been dreading for months, but he gave a truly great performance and in some miraculous way carried everyone in the cast with him in a superb display of unselfish acting.

A number of us had supper together at the hotel and he, Ken and I stayed talking for a long time after the others had left. It was clear that he had taken Ken's notes to heart and would act on them. It was slightly less than three weeks before the play opened in London and from then on Larry devoted himself to the production. He worked with Frank in private and rehearsed tirelessly himself with the company. At the same time he never impinged on John's position as director or ever took the credit away from him. Ever since the opening announcement of *Othello* the box-office had been inundated with demands for tickets. The seating problem had been a major headache from the beginning. In a typical English spirit the public had damned the venture before it started and were livid with rage when they couldn't obtain seats immediately it became a reality. In the letter columns of the papers they vented their disapproval of the forming of a National Theatre with 'their' money (which, by the way, is threepence per annum in the Greater London area and one penny per annum outside it) and renewed their poison-pen correspondence when they were unable to get tickets for *Othello*. One salient factor was ignored in the general brouhaha: the total seating capacity is only 878; the upper circle, gallery and standing places account for half this sum and a further number of seats have to be discounted for their poor visibility. By trial and error a system was devised to endeavour to satisfy the demand as fairly as possible by persuading people to book well in advance. The first postal response to this caught everyone by surprise. A mail van arrived and deposited its entire load into the Board Room with dozens of sacks of applications, which became a daily habit for some weeks. The secretaries volunteered to work overtime and help but soon every available body was lending a hand. Larry arrived very early one morning and asked me what was going on. I suggested he went in to see for himself. For an hour he sorted and filed until being eventually persuaded to go to his rehearsal.

The *Othello* first night built up to a crescendo of 'Quater-centennial Bard Idolatry' and the foyer was thronged. Standing to acknowledge the critics, I was fascinated by the audience. The National had inherited a gathering of old Old Vic enthusiasts known as the Vic-Wells Association: a number of these stalwarts had made themselves a little tiresome by their insistence on maintaining seats they had always occupied in the past. Two of these splendid old girls met each other by the box-office and chatted together. One said, 'It's not like the old days, is it dear, when we knew everybody?' The other answered gloomily, 'No—*he's* made it all different. I shan't stay till the end, it comes down too late.' Her chum sagely pointed out that the best of the play was contained in the last scenes but she was given the brush-off with 'That don't bother me, I've seen it before and I like to watch the telly in bed.' I longed to say to them that there had been offers of anything up to £100 per seat for the chance of being there that night, but refrained.

Next day the notices confounded the early doubts Larry had over playing the part: they were universal in their praise for his acting, although some presumed he had based his interpretation on a Negro. This misconception was a mere pinprick compared with the overall triumph.

I had my own two pairs of seats for every performance for press purposes and it was left to my discretion as to how they should be allocated. One morning I had a telephone call from the Russian Embassy explaining that a group of ten top Russian actors and directors were on a cultural visit to England and they wanted to see *Othello*. There had been vague murmurs that the company would go to Russia at some future date. I consulted Larry about the ticket problem. All the available house seats, plus mine, were pooled together, and I told the Cultural Attaché that we would accommodate them and issued an invitation for them to have a drink at the offices and meet Olivier before seeing him perform. Although they were bringing an interpreter with them Larry asked Mrs Sofka Skipwith, a White Russian who had been his secretary many years back, to translate for us. We had a little chat about the most suitable drink and came to the conclusion that, as good capitalists, we should serve champagne. This splendid gesture was wasted because in Russia it is the cheapest drink—whisky would have impressed them far more! On their arrival into the mews, heads peered out of the windows almost as if expecting men from Mars. Larry gave a welcoming toast and was slightly startled when he realised that the official interpreter was translating practically word by word, which was comic to watch. After a couple of sentences he stopped with an eyebrow raised, waiting for the translation before continuing the next bit. This was accompanied by a chorus of 'da's' and grunts of approval. Originally he had intended to 'say a few words' but it was obvious that only a lengthy speech would fit the occasion. Without interrupting I hastily went round and re-filled the glasses, including the speaker's who really looked as if he needed it. At last he managed to come to a graceful end with a flow of rhetoric which was greeted by a burst of applause and, I hoped, Russian 'bravos'. After a short interval for another drink it was the guests' turn to answer the toast. It finished half an hour later and we both clapped as hard as we could. Another bottle was opened and the atmosphere became less formal. I had some photographs of Larry as Othello for him to sign as mementos and, in exchange, the Russians solemnly presented him with snapshots of themselves which they had brought in their wallets. There was one actor who came from Georgia—tall, broad and very handsome—who was a famous Othello, the interpreter informed us. Without any sort of embarrassment he immediately threw himself into a scene—playing Othello and either Iago or Desdemona. We couldn't tell which as no one translated, but it was, literally, a shattering performance. Doors up the corridor flew open from fear of mayhem in the Board Room. This virtuoso display was acclaimed by the Russians with yells and stamping—in which Larry and I found ourselves joining. Then, as a gesture of goodwill, we all linked arms and sealed an Anglo-Russo pact of friendship by drinking in a circle out of each other's glasses. Very difficult and most of mine went down my cleavage. Two medals were swiftly pinned on our breasts to a burst of volga chorus and cheering which was continued down the corridor until we saw them into their cars. People surged into Larry's office demanding what the hell we had been up to but we were both too helpless with laughter to be able to give a coherent account except to say 'We have made some new friends!'

Although highly gratified by the success of *Othello* he soon realised what a terrifying exertion it put upon him. Each time he performed it he spent the morning at the gymnasium, had an early lunch of steak and half a bottle of red wine; then rested for a couple of hours before the marathon task of making up commenced, which took three and a half hours. He had given intensive thought to this which he had based on the North African Moor and, apart from varied shadings on his face, he didn't resort to tricks such as a false nose or cheek-padding to achieve the effect. I used to sit and talk to him while he made up and was always fascinated by it. Before coming to the theatre he would shave all superfluous hair; then, with his dresser's help, cover his entire body—leaving one notable exception—with a layer of liquid stain. When this had dried completely the operation was repeated with another coating of make-up containing some grease which was polished finally to give a sheen. He even painted his finger nails with a pale blue transparent varnish. The finished effect was stupendous. The job to remove it at the end of the show took an hour and a half. All this on top of the demands of the part tired him throughout the following day. Audiences, who were not aware of this, frequently complained he was 'only acting' and why couldn't he do it every day and allow more people to see it instead of being so grand. Little did they know what they were asking.

For many months there had been an undercurrent flowing between the younger generation of executives: the 'boys' and Ken. This became a sort of middle-aged child's game which I privately called 'taking sides'. From week to week it was impossible to know which way the triangle would side with the fourth angle, Larry. At the end of a normal working day—around six-thirty—either John or Bill, separately or sometimes together, would wander down my end of the corridor and go into Ken's room which was immediately opposite mine. Frequently these chats were concerned solely with the National plans but very often they developed into an attack against the Establishment (in this context meaning the Board and the Director). It was physically impossible not to hear these conversations because the partition walls were paper thin and the degree of audibility so clear it would make bats think they were deaf. I feel sure there was no spirit of malice in these little exchanges of opinion; they were more like a parlour-party-game called 'Power' instead of 'Monopoly'. They used to amuse me hugely because I never took them seriously.

But some of the amusement became more malicious when rehearsals started at Chichester. A number of young new recruits joined without having previously worked at the National or with Olivier and some of these were splendid material for anti-Establishment apartheid. Very soon it became apparent that there was divided loyalty in the company for the first time. Possibly this is unavoidable, though regrettable, in any organisation but the effect is more serious in a theatrical one which is primarily composed of egoists jockeying for position and voicing their stupid little opinions. During this period Larry and one half of the company were appearing in London; the only play he was concerned with that season was *Othello* which was the third production. I am convinced that some of the rumours that were going around had reached his ears and when he and the other section of the company arrived it was fascinating to feel the difference in the temperature; without any noticeable effort from him at least an outward unity was restored.

Back in London Larry asked me to go up to his office for a chat. I sat down and was slightly taken aback when he asked my opinion of Ken and whether he should be kept on—his contract was shortly coming up for renewal. I replied that I considered him to be very headstrong over many things and, because he had always been a lone wolf and unused to discipline, apt to use the National as a platform to air his own personal prejudices but that he was undoubtedly an asset to the organisation in his own sphere. When asked how I got on with him I answered that I found him a most amusing, if irresponsible, colleague whose windmill tilting I had now learned to live with. From Ken we went on to talk about the company generally. Larry is, above all, a born leader who really cares about actors and their work and, in turn, actors love working with him. We talked about their problems and he explained that there were two groups: those who feared being out of work due to family reasons or a need for security, and the others who took pleasure in not being tied down for any length of time preferring the danger of uncertainty. The idea of issuing long-term contracts in this country is relatively new and rare and he thought it would take a while before certain actors became accustomed to staying for three to five years before making a change. In the autumn darling Michael Redgrave, one of the original members of the company, was to be released to undertake a prior commitment to launch the Yvonne Arnaud Theatre at Guildford. One of his parts at the National was Solness in *The Master Builder*. Larry decided that he would take over this role and, as Maggie Smith was being over-worked by appearing in that, *Othello*, *The Recruiting Officer* and rehearsing for *Hay Fever*, a new policy was introduced for alternating parts. One half of the company was going out on the autumn tour while the other played in London. Joan Plowright was to share the role of Hilde with Maggie Smith and play it on the tour. Just before this started Joan, who had been acting in three productions, was taken ill and there were panic stations over her replacement. Maggie was appearing both in London and in some towns on the tour but couldn't be in two places at the same time. Concentrated rehearsals for *The Master Builder* started again with Jeanne Hepple as Hilde. Unfortunately this coincided with Jeanne, at Larry's earlier instigation, having all her teeth straightened and capped. We were faced with Joan's collapse, Maggie nearing a breakdown and Jeanne in agonies with the dentist. Only Larry appeared to be indefatigable, but it was becoming obvious that the pressure of work: the seemingly endless new plays, summer seasons and tours, were taking their toll on everyone. In spite of the brief holiday break for three weeks everybody was looking jaded and distraught. The National had presented eight productions plus a double-bill, made two provincial tours and a season at Chichester within twelve months of opening—all these under the most difficult conditions. Meanwhile protracted negotiations were going on over one of Ken's idées fixes. Ever since he had 'discovered' the Berliner Ensemble he had carried the torch for Brecht and was determined they should be seen again in this country in spite of the almost insuperable embargos on the East Berliners that were in effect at that time. Nothing daunted he yapped and harried at every conceivable source and made frequent trips to East Germany in his endeavours to get them over here.

Since the first year of the National the company's provincial tours had not achieved any great financial success.

The provinces seemed to have an in-built suspicion, imbued over the years, regarding the word 'tour'. To them it meant either a Prior-To-West-End-Try-It-Out-First-On-The-Dog or an After-West-End-Run—usually with a replacement cast. In the advance publicity it had been our policy to announce the names of the plays without drawing particular attention to any one actor: in other words implementing the non-star principle. This had bred even more scepticism in some of the different towns we had visited, with accompanying low audience attendance; in fact more so since we presented two plays during one week to which they were totally unaccustomed. Larry, with his commercial theatre upbringing, was cross and baffled by this apparent lack of enthusiasm and determined to overcome it. Two days before the opening in Glasgow of the 1965 Spring Tour with *Hay Fever* (which had been acclaimed with rave notices by the national and provincial press when it had first opened in London), he suddenly asked me if I would go up to Scotland and, as he put it, lay on everything possible—and to bring David, my husband, and our two dogs as well! I telephoned every known contact in Glasgow, Edinburgh and the surrounding district to arrange an informal press party in the dress-circle bar for Monday morning to be followed up with various television and press interviews throughout the week. Larry flew up for that evening performance and a sleeper had been booked to take him back to London after the show, on the same train by which we were travelling. David and I had had a cold snack and an instruction from Larry that we should obtain some drinks for the long return journey. At that time his preference was for whisky and we duly sought the help of the hotel barman who, on hearing Olivier's name, produced from behind his counter a bottle of one of the Glen whiskies with a pale primrose hue. This, together with our own tipple, we took onto the train. The two of us had an intercommunicating compartment which we opened—giving us an over-all space of at most three foot from bed to bed. Larry brought with him the repertory manager and the production manager. At once the compartments resembled one of the Marx Brothers' films: the four men sat on David's bed; the two Yorkshire terriers, Barbara and Abigail, sat on mine; I squatted on the floor in the intervening twelve-inch space between the doors and being the smallest, dispensed the drinks. Larry was delighted with his first straw whisky and, after a few miles, eagerly accepted a re-fill. By the time Carlisle had been passed, accompanied by a few more strong libations and mildly scurrilous conversation, it seemed to be time for bed. Larry, who appeared to be sober as a judge, raised himself from the bed. He was thrown by the lurch of the train and sank back again but, after the third attempt, it became rather clear that his legs were refusing to obey his head. Giggling helplessly he appealed to us to agree that he couldn't possibly be tight on three drinks, could he? We disagreed on this point and the three men volunteered to escort him to his own sleeper two compartments away. This was more difficult than it sounded because by now the train had gathered enormous speed and, from the waist down, Larry's legs seemed to consist of india-rubber. Noisily bumping and boring along the corridor he was safely seen into his own berth. Next morning, on Euston station, a radiant-faced Larry said to us accusingly 'I'm *still* tight!' This was the first and only time I have ever seen him the worse for alcohol—and it was probably due to lack of food and highly proofed whisky.

In the New Year Arthur Miller's witch-hunt play *The Crucible* was presented and directed by Larry. It had had a lukewarm reception when produced at the Royal Court a few years earlier but luckily the critics were most enthusiastic about the National revival. Miller was in Paris and arranged to fly over to see the second performance. With his consent I had arranged a press party for him the following day. The journalists were complimentary about *The Crucible* but they started to grill him on the subject of *After the Fall*, his latest play dealing, supposedly, with his ex-wife Marilyn Monroe. He parried their questions with charm, courtesy and impersonality, but over lunch in Larry's office he unbent and described Miss Monroe as 'a living doll and a complete neurotic'. To which Larry heartily agreed, having worked with her on the film *The Prince and the Showgirl*. Larry related an incident that had occurred in Monaco: he and Joan were dining with the Rainiers in the Palace one night and it became obvious that His Royal Highness was becoming bored and seemed to be nodding off. Searching in his mind for a topic to enliven the conversation he hit on the filming with Marilyn Monroe. Suddenly he realised that the original play—in which he had appeared—was entitled *The Sleeping Prince* and he hastily discarded that and launched into his little anecdote. When asked the name of the film he was on the point of uttering it but in the nick of time saw the anomaly of *The Prince and the Showgirl* and, with some confusion, confessed he had forgotten. I expect they would have thought it as funny as we did.

At a meeting I was told definitely we were to visit Moscow and West Berlin in the summer; this in addition to a spring tour, a season at Chichester followed by a long autumn tour after the foreign visit. Strings were still being pulled to bring over the Berliner Ensemble and other visiting companies to occupy the Old Vic during the late summer. All this looked a tough programme and proved so for some of the actors. The repertoire became to complicated that a special play timetable was posted on all the notice boards. One of the worst hit was Maggie Smith: although she was released from two of her roles she was still appearing in two plays and frequently left the Old Vic to catch a plane for Scotland returning the same night on a sleeper to be on the National stage the next day. I christened the company's itinerary a 'commution' it was so tortuous.

While the spring tour was continuing it was already necessary to decide the programme for Chichester: this was to include a double-bill of two contrasting one-act plays starring Maggie Smith and Albert Finney. Strindberg's *Miss Julie* was chosen for the first play but nobody could agree on the choice of the comedy to accompany it. Hundreds of one-acters were read and discarded; meanwhile the announcement of the plans for the season were long overdue. An epic play by Peter Shaffer, *The Royal Hunt of the Sun*, had been presented at Chichester the previous year and was highly successful both there and later at the National. Someone—probably Ken—hit on the brilliant idea of asking Peter to write a comedy for us. Maintaining that he had never written to order, very, very reluctantly he was 'persuaded' to agree. There was, however, a small hitch: he could not think of a plot! I issued a bold statement that 'Peter Shaffer will be the author of a new play at Chichester at present untitled.' That was the *under*statement of all time. Peter was due to fly to America and the days were running out. A few evenings before leaving he, John Dexter and Kenneth Tynan went out to supper and later in a taxi the idea for *Black Comedy* was born. We had a title, a vague plot and not one word of dialogue. It was offered to two directors who turned it down with scorn but John—sportingly—agreed to produce the non-existent masterpiece and started rehearsing the small cast. The basic idea was inspired by the Chinese Classical

Theatre in which two heavily armed combatants fight supposedly in the dark although the lights are full up. John,
sensibly, realised that they would need extensive rehearsing
to accustom themselves to 'playing in the dark'. After a
week he received the first draft outline, but no dialogue. This
put the actors further in the dark and it was returned with
fresh suggestions. Backwards and forwards went the correspondence and the actors went on crawling and fumbling
round the stage not knowing what their characters were
meant to be. At last a script arrived, Maggie's reaction was
typical of her: she was greatly relieved because she had
thought Peter had meant her to be a man.

It had been agreed that Larry should have some time off to
make a film and, in his absence, the administration was
conducted by John, Bill and Ken in consultation with
Kenneth Rae and George Rowbottom (the General Manager)
with ultimate reference to Larry himself. The rivalry between the three 'boys' was becoming more overt and one
could never be quite sure which was on speaking terms
with the other two. They were getting restless and seeking
either more authority or other outlets. Bill came in for a drink
one evening and confessed he would rather administrate or
teach young actors than produce and that he was having
meetings with George Devine about the possibility of taking
over the administration of the Royal Court when George
retired because of ill-health. Ken was in a state of frustration
because the go-ahead had not yet been given for labour permits for his beloved Berliner Ensemble. Much of his time
was given over to lobbying and telephoning the Right People
to speed up the formalities and conducting a brisk letter
campaign in the press pointing out that Art knows no

Check-Point-Charlie barriers. I, too, was doing a little machinating. Ever since being told the Moscow trip was official I determined to go all out to publicise it. It was my intention to take some of our leading English critics with us to report the first foreign openings but before approaching the individual papers I had to make sure that visas and accommodation would be available to them. Since the Russian actors' visit I had established very good relationships with their Embassy and they were most helpful and co-operative. Just before the USSR May Day celebrations I had a strange telephone call from a woman journalist in Moscow asking, in fairly good English, if I could get a message for the Russian people from Larry. I promised to do my best and asked her to telephone again the following day. Without bothering him I composed a stirring piece breathing amity, unity, peace, love and light and dictated it to her next day which cemented a friendly newspaper contact for the tour. Another dotty scheme I dreamed up was to find an organisation willing, for publicity, to provide a wardrobe for the more important members of the company. I approached the Wool Secretariat who agreed to do it with two provisos: firstly all the recipients should be photographed during fittings in London and secondly they intended engaging a newsreel unit, at their own expense, to accompany us and expected the actors to make themselves available for filming and photographs in Moscow wearing the clothes provided. This put me in a tight spot. I couldn't really see Larry going all the way with that little plan. I chose my moment and ingenuously asked him if he would like six new suits for free. 'My darling girl, who wouldn't? What's the catch?' I briefly outlined the scheme. He replied that it would be unfair to the others if he agreed. I assured him that, in fact, *if* he agreed eleven other actors would also benefit. This delighted him and he gave in at once. I seized the opportunity and nonchalantly said he might have to be photographed a few times but I think he elected not to hear that bit.

At last a decision had been reached regarding the Berliner Ensemble: they were to give a three-week season at the Vic during August 1965, just before we left for Russia. For the next few weeks there was frenetic bustle mixed with a considerable degree of confusion in all departments: scenery and costumes to be transported to Russia—no, not Chichester, RUSSIA—arrangements for scenery and costumes to be sent from *East* Berlin to England, and England to *West* Berlin; programmes translated into Russian and German, conversely from German into English; visas, passports, work permits; explaining to the Germans that children under the age of twelve were not allowed on the stage in this country, remembering to allocate a chaperone for the two youngsters we were taking abroad . . . daily the problems multiplied. Nerves were getting frayed, tempers flared and little ploys were hatching up and down the corridor.

Whenever Larry's car entered the mews, office doors would pop open, someone's voice would yell 'He's here!' and a knot of people with various queries would line up in the corridor for priority to see him. This apparently unavoidable procedure was a strain both for him and for those waiting on his decision. Through lack of time he often had three or four people together in his office which sometimes caused a certain amount of embarrassment if the problem was in any way private. I suppose it must demand too much from human nature to be unwillingly classed as a genius and generally treated with universal adulation without tending to fall into an autonomous trap. Whether he enjoys it or not— or is even aware of it, which is very open to doubt—one cannot judge.

5

Moscow: The first foreign tour

FOR THE Moscow/Berlin tour we were taking three plays: *Othello* and *Hobson's Choice* from the repertoire and, as a mad bravura gesture 'opening cold' with a new production of *Love for Love*. This had already been rehearsing for a number of weeks and it was scheduled to give everyone going abroad three weeks' holiday in July before the final rehearsals prior to the tour. Larry chose to stay, unofficially, in Brighton to spend all his time with the children. With the company away I settled down with a sigh of relief to the forthcoming Berliner Ensemble and the routine chores of Chichester, which had already opened in July. After the first night of *Arturo Ui* a party was given in the dress-circle bar by the Board for Bertolt Brecht's widow, Helene Weigel, and the Ensemble. Frau Weigel could not understand why Larry and the great aficionado Ken were absent. It was explained that Larry was having an enforced holiday before the arduous tour and that Ken was, unfortunately, in the States on business. During the second week, after all four plays had been launched, a large party was held in the Vic rehearsal room. Numerous actors from other theatres were invited and the charming and gregarious host was the Chairman, Lord Chandos. I stood near him and helped with various introductions. When Helli Weigel arrived she ceremoniously presented me with a beautiful gold brooch from Germany. Although charmed by the gesture and the gift I couldn't avoid the feeling that she had not originally purchased it with *me* in mind; nevertheless I was delighted and proud to receive it. Some days later, after much hospitality from the East Berliners, I felt it was incumbent for someone to play host to the visitors on behalf of the National Theatre Company and suggested to the Chichester contingent that we should invite them down for an evening. This idea was taken up enthusiastically by Maggie Smith, Albert Finney and Robert Stephens, with Maggie as chief organiser. She personally cooked a splendid cold supper and all the company chipped in, as much as they could afford, for lashings of drink. We hired a private bus and I escorted them down. Immediately the audience had left the foyer was quickly transformed into a party room with Albie's hi-fi playing Western pop. Few of the cast spoke German and few of the guests English but it didn't matter. In a short space of time all of us, including our Cockney driver, were having a ball. As we left for London in the early hours the cast crowded round the bus singing and cheering the guests. On the long drive home they talked of nothing except the play, the acting and, above all, the warm welcome they had received from the National Company. I know it went a long way to alleviate any feeling they might have had that they had been snubbed. On their last night they played *Coriolan* with Helene Weigel as Volumnia. Much to her delight Larry came up for this performance and she received him in his own dressing-room which he had asked to be put at her disposal. The Ensemble were flying back the following day but Helli was travelling alone two days later. As a courtesy I accompanied her to the airport where her plane was delayed for three hours: we sat and talked. She told me she was flying to a clinic for treatment, and that she had been ill throughout her stay in England. She talked a lot about Larry: she told me how much she admired him and how concerned she felt over his apparent indifference towards her Company, adding with a smile that she realised everyone was not necessarily a Brecht disciple. I hotly denied this and tried to explain the supreme personal effort involved in forming the National Theatre, and that this in conjunction with the ardours of the forthcoming foreign tour made it imperative that he should have a holiday—which had indeed been forced upon him. Helli viewed me in silence for a few moments with a twinkle in her eye and eventually said 'Virginia, you are a very loyal girl; your Olivier is a very great man but, au fond, he is only a man. I am older than he is and feel like a mother towards him because he has behaved a little badly and he knows it and that hurts him.' God knows! Larry does not have to defend his actions, but I wished, fervently, that he instead of me had had this conversation. Realising the importance of the Ensemble's visit I further wished I had tried harder to persuade him to be present in his official capacity at the opening, or one of the three first nights, so avoiding this speculation. It is so ridiculous the number of times I, and others with personal feelings for him, neglected to pursue a subject to which he appeared to be antipathetic by reassuring one's self that 'He's got too much on his mind and shouldn't be further worried.' This was never done through fear but from a misplaced motive not to add to his responsibilities and his already over-taxed strength. The question of priorities always came uppermost and, in many instances, were wrongly chosen.

For the last weeks of rehearsal for *Love For Love* we hired the Scala Theatre to devote all available time to this production as it had not been played in the repertoire. Ten days before our departure Larry was suddenly taken ill with another 'virus infection' which appeared to take the same form as the previous illness. His doctors were fairly sanguine that it could be treated and he would be able to undertake the tour. His understudy took over rehearsals for the role and the working schedule was intensified. Fears were not so much that he would be unfit to play in *Love For Love*—which is a team play—but that he might not be well enough to appear in *Othello*, the highlight of the tour. An emergency meeting was called to discuss what should be done: cancel it (the tour) or chance his health. Fortunately Larry had earlier decided to take Joan with us (at his own expense) knowing there would be innumerable functions when she could deputise for him. Privately, as his wife, her presence would be invaluable. It was decided to go ahead providing the doctors' report was satisfactory within the next two days. At the end of the week, with Larry still away, a representative from the Foreign Office came to give us a 'behaviour briefing'. This was attended by the press and cameramen who were accompanying us. Joan was present and Larry's absence was remarked on by them. Backed up by her I said he had a feverish cold which they accepted. We were then given a lecture ending with some cautionary warnings which sounded so Bondishly sinister that none of us took them seriously. It was stressed that even though part of the hotel-restaurant was reserved for us exclusively, we should all guard our speech since the tables would certainly be miked and this also applied to Larry's suite and the rooms occupied by me and the press. There were lots of other dark hints such as 'No woman should wear more than one wedding ring'. That struck me as plumb dotty. I frequently wear five or six and what the hell has that to do with good relationships with the USSR. Anyway my press chums and I went out to the pub to have a good giggle about the awful pitfalls we had been advised to avoid!

The following week Larry returned to work looking fit and well. We were flying that weekend and on arrival at London Airport it seemed to be swarming with the National Theatre. After seeing Larry through endless television and newspaper interviews we made our way to the departure lounge which looked like a jumble sale. Dozens of actors were lining up at a portion of the duty-free shop which had been reserved for the National group and were buying liquor and cigarettes in bulk as if preparing for a long siege and the lounge echoed with their voices sounding like the parrot house in the Zoo. As we reached the chartered Viscount we were greeted at the top of the boarding steps by an impertinent and over-familiar captain—Larry. He had seized a jacket and cap belonging to one of the crew and was gaily welcoming us aboard. We joked as all the booze was being loaded into the hold and prepared to wave to our loved ones at take-off. After an hour our enthusiasm waned. Two hours later, still on the ground and gasping for air, the whole project assumed an air of total unreality. Larry suggested they had forgotten to put an engine into the damned thing; someone else said it was a dirty trick engineered by one of the Royal Shakespeare Company. We took off two and a quarter hours late, very hot and very thirsty.

The flight lasted seven hours and it was pitch dark when

we touched down. The first Russian contact was with the custom officials who smilingly welcomed us and waved everyone through without opening any of the luggage. This gesture was a privilege for the Company. A battery of floodlights blinded us as we emerged and cameras filmed our arrival. Masses of people, all carrying bouquets of flowers, moved towards us and tried to introduce themselves. Many of them were actors from the Moscow Art Theatre and darling George Rowbottom, our General Manager, who had flown over a few days previously with a number of our technical staff. Tired from the journey and overwhelmed by the reception we started to pile into the waiting coaches. The one I was in started to drive off but was prevented by a 'charming' airport official waving his arms and letting forth an obvious flow of abuse. He threw the door open and screamed at us. Through an interpreter it appeared that the customs had concluded all the passengers were part of the Company and, on examining the passports, discovered members of the press and Pathé Newsreel cameramen were also aboard. They extricated the nine 'suspects' and proceeded to search them thoroughly for half an hour. Eventually we were allowed to leave and arrived, starving hungry and utterly exhausted, at our hotel. There further complications: for weeks they had known the number of rooms required but there weren't sufficient available to accommodate everyone. Leaving an interpreter and George to try and sort it out we had some much needed food—it was one o'clock in the morning—and the lucky ones went to bed. The Ukraine Hotel, a mock Gothic monstrosity built a few years ago, has a curious lift system. There is one lift block that serves half the building but only goes to the ninth floor; facing this is another that registers twenty-four floors but, in operation, doesn't go further than the seventeenth—the one I had been allotted. Arriving up in the eyrie I realised there were two beds in the huge room but, in unsporting fashion I decided to keep that information to myself. Next morning I was woken by the telephone and a stream of Russian; foolishly I replied in French, being the only other language I can speak, inwardly cursing that I had not got an interpreter with me. The woman's voice changed to pidgin English. 'Me meet Hamlet Olivier—write for paper, da?' From which I inferred that she was a journalist and wanted an interview. 'Da, Kremlevsky Theatre' I replied and quickly hung up and started to get dressed. Zoë Dominic, the well-known photographer who we had asked to accompany us, had been to Russia previously and advised me take some instant coffee with me, plus a tiny triangular arrangement, some packets of solid methylated tablets to heat it and a large metal thimble to extinquish it. All highly primitive but it proved a godsend because there is no room service and the nearest 'byfyet' was three floors away. Feeling like an incendiary, I lit the infernal machine and inspected the bathroom. It was very modern and well-equipped—although lacking a plug for the handbasin—not because it had been lost or broken but simply that plugs are not considered necessary in basins, which was borne out by the superior one attached to the bath. This is a false premise because it's damn well impossible to wash one's face, shampoo your hair or do 'the smalls' without one. As a precaution I had brought a universal plug which was to be in constant demand for hair-do's and laundry and subsequently left for another fellow traveller. A hot bath, a steaming mug of coffee, dressed—and no telephone calls—I proceeded on the perilous journey to find Larry. At the end of the corridor, immediately facing the lifts, was a bureau-desk behind which was seated an imposing lady of the Soviet Union, the receiver of the room keys. These guardian angels are stationed in strategic positions on every floor and it is virtually impossible to retain the key to your own room. Humbly submitting mine I sat down on a 'love seat' encircling a pillar (thoughtfully provided with a mass of cultural literature) and waited for the lift to arrive. I later discovered that dropping in to Larry's room from mine could take anything up to twenty minutes to achieve!

After a struggle and some grim determination I arrived in Larry's suite; a bedroom, bathroom and sitting room all lavishly Victorian with yards of coy frilly net curtains and green bobble-fringed table cloths. Neither of them were dressed, but in very gay form. To my chagrin I saw a trolley with breakfast. 'How did you get that?' I demanded. 'Because, dear Ginny, you may remember I have not been well—and it's the only bloody reason they'll accept for room service.' Pointing up to the ceiling I reminded him that THEY might be listening. He gravely agreed that I was quite right and he hoped he would be 'well' soon, adding that he was a dirty capitalist and going to make the most of it. I told him about my telephone call and he said Nina, the interpreter who had been seconded to him, would meet us at the theatre and help to cope.

We got into the chauffeur-driven car that had been hired for his use and set out for the theatre. It is situated within the Kremlin walls, next door to the Palace of Congress, and this was the first time any foreign company had ever acted in it. Leaving the car in Red Square we climbed some steps and made our way to the front of the theatre. George had left two formidable passes to enable us to go through the stage door. Larry's interpreter was also there together with the persistent lady journalist to whom he gave a brief interview. The two of us then proceeded backstage. We came to a vast iron gate and prodded it open—as it swung back we were confronted by a sentry who was a veritable walking arsenal. He pointed an ominous lethal weapon at us and, quivering, we brandished our passes and were allowed through. We walked onto the stage and were greeted by Diana Boddington, the unflappable Stage Manager, saying to one of her underlings, 'Go and find George, darling, and tell him Larry's here.' Within seconds he came over looking very long-faced and told us what was going on.

КРЕМЛЕВСКИЙ
ТЕАТР

НАЦИОНАЛЬНЫЙ ТЕАТР
ВЕЛИКОБРИТАНИИ

1965 г.   АРТИСТИЧЕСКИЙ

In London, during negotiations, we had stipulated that no performance should be broadcast or televised. This had delayed the final signatures but the point had ultimately been conceded and incorporated into the contract. The stage staff were working in the theatre and someone spotted a battery of television cameras placed round the dress circle converging on the stage. George was informed and he called an emergency meeting of the heads of staff of the National and the heads of Gosconcert, who were presenting us on behalf of the Soviet government. This was still in session in an ante-room off-stage. When we entered the little room it was thick with smoke and stubbornness—not helped by the language barrier. There were two interpreters but none of the English were in a position to know how accurately they were being interpreted. After a few minutes Larry whispered to me to take his car and go back to tell our press. My mind was so concentrated on the crisis that I had completely forgotten our chum at the gate, passes or passwords. He put his hand out to halt me and, without thinking, I shook it and wished him 'Good morning'. He seemed very surprised, roared with laughter—he had the most beautiful blue eyes I've seen—opened the gate for me and waved as I left. Luckily I saw Barry Norman of the *Daily Mail* and Felix Barker of the *Evening News* buying postcards in the lobby: I grabbed them and went out for a little stroll while I related the saga. It was now past noon and we went to the restaurant to hear the latest development. There we found everyone in a state of frenetic confusion, every department seemed to have an insurmountable problem: at dawn a freight plane had arrived with baskets containing costumes and props; these were loaded onto lorries, transported to the theatre, opened and dumped in the courtyard. Nobody in the theatre was told of their arrival, there had been a violent rainstorm and everything was saturated with water. The stage staff, who had flown two days in advance of the Company to set-up *Othello* throughout Sunday, were faced with a Russian folk-dance group performing that night. They, with stalwart Russian stage hands, started to shift the dance company's scenery out at one-thirty and worked solidly through the night setting up *Othello*. This meant the loss of a much needed day-and-a-half vital rehearsal time for us to get accustomed to a foreign routine—Larry's gloomy reaction was that he doubted very much whether it would even be 'all right on the night'. The scenic painters had met with a firm 'Nyet' when they tried to repaint some of the permanent backcloths, and the carpenters an even firmer one when they sought permission to widen a door-way to enable the actors to arrive on the stage with their costumes in one piece! The earlier television threat almost paled into insignificance but, in context, it was part of the pattern of behaviour that we were determined somehow to overcome, making every allowance for ignorance of Western procedure.

Having finished the 'sludgy' lunch—all the food looked and tasted grey—the Company, with faces the colour of the food they had just eaten, left for the theatre to rehearse well into the night. Larry had given me the sort of instructions I would have had in England: deal with all press enquiries, no interviews and no pictures until after the opening. Disconsolately I went up to my room and took stock of my own situation. Since it had been agreed I should go on tour, I felt someone had slipped up through not thinking of giving me my own interpreter. If anybody made a balls of finding their way round the Metro it was their own personal gaffe; I couldn't afford to make one. However, I was there and, somehow, had to do my job. I had already noticed one baffling omission in the Soviet way of life: there were no telephone books and no way of discovering a number. All enquiries were greeted by bland ignorance. I had brought with me the number of my sole contact, Anya, who I knew worked for a magazine. In despair I telephoned her and asked if she would be allowed to come and help me for a few hours which she said she could do. Journalists were waiting in the reception hall demanding Larry. Anna brought six up with her, two could speak halting English and, while I dealt with them, she answered the telephone. One represented the official radio and, to my horror, I heard myself consenting to give an interview to the USSR in place of Larry. Anya guided me through. Shortly after eight we called a halt and had a well-earned imported brandy—a great rarity in Moscow. She joined me for dinner and promised she would assist me as much as she was able.

I woke next morning with the sort of sick-excited feeling I used to have as a child before a party. With a bang I remembered what day it was. In the bath I tried to reassure myself that every seat for the season had been sold in advance but it only made my stomach more queasy. The actors had the morning free but the poor stage management, electricians and technicians had an early call. Before my phone started I went down to the theatre: the cameras were still there but would only be filming during the reception at the curtain call; the backcloths were being painted; the door enlarged and the costumes were being artificially dried. I hardly recognised our team: they seemed to have aged years over-night—some of the lads had four days growth of beard—but they were less depressed than doggedly determined. I returned to my bedroom and an interpreter, Vladimir, a young man with antediluvian silent-screen ideas of seduction was lent to me for a couple of hours—ostensibly to take calls and translate. One call seemed to baffle him and he passed it to me saying, 'This one not Russian, it is a foreign lady.' I took the phone tentatively and a booming American voice asked to speak to Virginia Fairweather. I replied she was doing so and a second boom said, 'Well hello there, this is Ethel Merman!' I knew Moscow was Madsville but this was going too far. I asked how I could help her and she said she had just arrived in Moscow, had got two seats for the open-ing through Larry and he'd suggested her contacting me—as an arbiter of fashion! What should she wear? I could only hint that any old jeans would pass muster, minks were two a rouble but, when in doubt go for the little black number. With a final boom of 'Thank you, dear Emily Post,' she hung up. I thanked her, dear Ethel Merman, for releasing some of my nervous tension and for making me laugh at the incongruity of the situation. I laughed even more later when I met her in Larry's room: she had dressed down and still managed to look like a well-decorated Christmas tree.

The press and I left together for the theatre in a heavy shower. Taxis were very scarce and Felix had an ignominious scuffle with an outraged Muscovy duck and won. The curtain was not due to rise for an hour but the Kremlin was packed with people. They were swarming round the theatre and begging for tickets. The doors were closed and I escorted my friends through the tiny box-office space into the vast marble auditorium leading off it. This is about a hundred yards in length with busts and photographs of all their notable actors and playwrights—reminiscent of the Comédie Française without the opulence. Outside we could see the crowds queueing for admission. There were only two hefty women 'usherettes' and when they opened the doors to let in the huge audience it was clear they couldn't cope. After a few minutes' animated shoving they gave up the struggle and deserted, leaving the foyer a seething mass. The curtain was late because they were still arguing backstage. At the very last moment the television cameramen had taken their places and were planning to film the play. George was making it plain that we had no intention of taking the curtain up unless the cameras were removed altogether—it had now become apparent, perhaps, that the Russians did not fully comprehend an English 'No!' However, a compromise was reached: one of our team would sit with their Russian compatriot until the end of the show when they could film whatever they liked. This was agreed and, at long last, the auditorium doors were opened, the audience flooded in, found their own seats, quietly settled down and waited for the curtain to rise. I rushed backstage to wish them luck and a very tired Diana Boddington said, 'Oh, Ginny, I'm so glad you're here darling —there are a bunch of your photographers in my prompt corner who are going to take pictures during the show— Larry says can you send them away, darling?' Taking a deep breath I walked into the wings and found a dozen of the biggest toughs I've ever seen with cameras. Turning on what persuasive charm I could I grabbed one by the arm and took him through the pass door into a passage. Luckily the others followed. Shouting 'Wait!' I went back to the wings and yanked one of the interpreters with me. Without any inner conviction I explained that unmentionable horrors would befall them if they took *one* picture while the play was on but I would give them every help if they met me at the end of the show. It was a soap-opera performance but it worked. I guided the lot back through the packed auditorium to a corridor with a cloakroom just off the stalls where I insisted on them depositing their cameras and, by dumbshow, pointed to a clock and made them understand that was where I would meet them at the end. Quietly I went into the back of the theatre and stood with George to watch the opening scenes. Russians are so familiar with Shakespeare that he does not need translation but there was an audible gasp on Larry's first entrance because they had never before seen such a real characterisation. We crept out of the auditorium and went up to the circle level to have a drink. This was the same size as the ground floor foyer and, facing the outer wall, there were a row of display counters with open sandwiches of caviar or smoked swordfish and quarter bottles of champagne, vodka, wine and beer displayed on each. George bought two quart bottles of champagne and a couple of heaped caviar sand-

9a

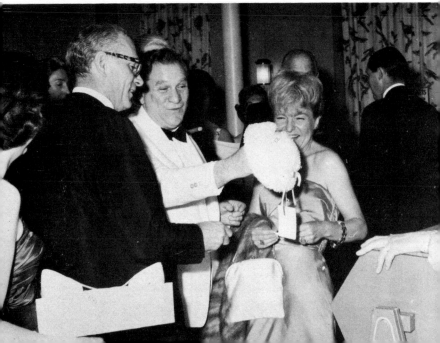

9b

10a

10b

12a

12b

wiches—for which he paid the equivalent of ten shillings—
and we toasted the night and the season. Not knowing the
theatre-going customs, but remembering the English habits,
I ordered the same for the interval for the press. Stationing
myself at the stalls exit I conducted them upstairs to my
newly found price right store. Doubting whether my earlier
dumb show had sunk in any more deeply than the television
episode I wandered downstairs and took up my vigil in front
of the cloakroom. There was one solitary photographer—
there always is. There was three-quarters of an hour still to
go and I realised that, if I kept up a smiling, nodding acquain-
tance with this gentleman until then, I might easily find
myself a St. Vitus's dance sufferer. Letting him get his beloved camera out of pawn I seized his arm and took him into
the hushed auditorium. He stood transfixed, occasionally
squeezing my hand with emotion and, ugly and black-
toothed as he was, I loved him. Knowing by the text that the
end was near, I gestured to him to wait for me and slipped
out to the corridor. Word had got around and there were at
least thirty jolly photographers and with finger on lips I
enjoined them to silence. I had earlier arranged with Zoë
Dominic and Douglas Warth (of Pathé) to take the left-hand
aisle leaving the right—which led to the pass-door—clear for
me. I summoned them to the entrance and when I heard
'this heavy act with heavy heart relate' I opened the door
and, feeling bloody silly, marshalled my little gang straight
down to the edge of the stage in deathly silence. Suddenly
the applause broke out in a mounting, unbelievable storm.
Hundreds who had been sitting in the circle vacated their
seats which snapped back like thunder and joined those in the
stalls, everyone surging towards the stage yelling and cheering at the same time. There was curtain after curtain with the
audience pelting the actors with flowers. I noticed that 'my'

photographers were on the stage at the side of the bowing actors, but nothing seemed to matter any more. After fifteen minutes of continuous applause Larry put up his hand for silence. This moment was ill-chosen by two impassive six-foot tall men to walk slowly onto the stage bearing a ten-foot high floral edifice which they proceeded to place in front of him—completely blotting him from view. Bewilderment was written all over his face as this procession advanced but, with great aplomb, he went 'with' the situation and waited until they had left. He then peered through the thing to gales of laughter, walked round it and gave a short speech in perfect Russian that he had previously learnt. This caused the already emotional audience to go mad: total strangers embraced each other—this did not exclude the frigid English —and with tear-stained faces we went backstage to salute Larry and the National who had brought about this triumph.

The first person we saw was Diana Boddington in a flood of tears. Thinking this was emotional relief, like ours, I sent her up and said crying was fashionable tonight. She rounded on me and said it was all very well for me to joke but Larry had just come off the stage and given her hell because some of the lighting cues had been wrong. In fact, dog tired, she had been struggling the whole evening between our staff, the Russian staff and the interpreters who had not conveyed her instructions fast enough and had frequently countermanded them by accident. We assured her that it had been magnificently smooth technically and went to Larry's room. He already had a glass of champagne in his hand and we offered our congratulations. He replied that they should be reserved for 'having got through the show at all', but he was quite overcome by the unprecedented reception. He confessed he had dreaded the world-famous Kremlin chimes—the huge cathedral bells that ring every quarter—would strike during the pause following the line 'Silence that dreadful bell!' adding that if it had he would have said '*and* that one too.' He was highly complimented on his Russian speech and he told us that the 'entrance of the gladiators' had nearly thrown him because, taken unawares, he forgot momentarily the opening phrase and he had learnt it parrot fashion! Madame Furtseva, the Russian Minister of Culture, some of the leading members of the Moscow Art Theatre—and Ethel Merman—crowded into the room to pay homage. The Company had been invited to a party at the British Embassy after the show and the invitation extended to the press travelling with us. Barry Norman had to go back to the hotel to phone through his copy for the following morning's paper but would join us immediately he had got the call.

Embassy parties tend to have a routine monotony but this one proved the exception: Sir Geoffrey Harrison, the new Ambassador, and his staff welcomed us, genuinely, and made us feel at home. And—after only three days—it was a wonderful relief to talk to strangers who could understand each other. Everyone soon made their way to the long dining-table, groaning with hot and cold food that was very different from our sludge, and proceeded to serve themselves. Piling our plates like school children, Jack Lambert, of the *Sunday Times*, Felix Barker and I caught up with poor Diana, now dry-eyed and looking cheerful. Suddenly she espied Miss Jennie Lee, who was on a short cultural visit, a few yards away; she moved over to her and said how honoured and thrilled she was to meet her, adding that she herself was married to a Welshman whose great idol had been Aneurin Bevan. There was a second's silence and then, with a steely look from her very lovely eyes, Miss Lee answered that she did not like anyone to mention her husband's name. Diana blushed scarlet, tried to stammer something and then burst into tears again! We three quickly engaged our Minister of Culture in polite conversation to allow Diana to retreat. Lord Thomson of Fleet was another unexpected guest; Larry, assuming he had been in the audience, asked him if he had enjoyed the play. Rather to his surprise, he enquired 'What play?' On hearing the answer he laughed and confided that he preferred shows with under-clad girlies. Larry replied with tongue in cheek that he might have enjoyed *his* performance since he stripped to the buff and was coloured black into the bargain. In the salon one of the actors played the piano—in the absence of a balalaika—and everyone danced. In the midst of the high spirits there was a telephone call for me; it was dear Barry Norman stuck in the hotel without food or transport. I told the Ambassador this sad story and, although the kitchens were closed, his chef packed up a wonderful 'picnic hamper' for me to take back to him. It looked like a wedding cake covered with silver foil and there were some very dirty cracks on the way home in the bus. Nothing daunted I rang Barry's room and he slipped up to mine trying hard to evade the eagle eye of the custodian— any evening room-visiting is strictly frowned on in the USSR. While he devoured the food he told me that he had been unable to get a taxi because it was 'after ten-thirty!' As the curtain had come down about then it didn't appear to make much sense but we were already beginning to realise that non-sense seemed to be the rule.

Next day, in the *Evening News*, Felix Barker ended his piece by saying 'As I made my way back through the empty streets of the city, memories of the huge success that our National Theatre has won with its first performance was wonderfully gratifying. If ever an actor can claim, in the world of the theatre: "I have done the State some service", he is Laurence Olivier.'

We all met at lunch time in the restaurant. Felix had been to the children's department store and bought the current vogue toy: this was a moon missile which one filled with water and 'pressurised' by an ingenious pump with a trigger-attachment for firing. This intrigued Larry immediately. He solemnly followed verbal instructions and, pointing upwards, released the catch. The thing shot into the air, hit the ornate painted ceiling, dislodged lumps of plaster before falling on a table and breaking four plates and a couple of glasses! This display had been watched with grave interest by the waiter and interpreters. On its crash landing it was greeted by a burst of applause from them and 'God that's torn it!' from Larry. Sweet, contrary people the Russians who insisted that he should try again for bigger and better effects—quite oblivious that a certain amount of damage was being done to their beautiful ceiling!

This was the second opening night *Hobson's Choice*—Larry had a free day before dress rehearsing the following morning for *Love For Love*. He suggested that I should go to the theatre for the start of *Hobson* and then join him for drinks later. I watched the first half of the play which was accompanied by the 'instantaneous interpretation' given by Larry's Nina seated in the box, with the low buzz coming through the headphones attached to the seats. This play written by Harold Brighouse in 1916, appealed to the audience who seemed to recognise its spirit of revolution and they laughed and applauded without bothering to use their headphones.

I returned to the hotel and went up to Larry's suite; he had ordered a massive bowl of iced caviar and some champagne. We sat and talked about our reactions to this strange country that we felt we had lived in for years instead of days. He gave me a hair-raising account of being driven to the Embassy the previous night. The streets were almost deserted—there is no night life and no bars open—an elderly man weaved across the road in front of them. Instead of swerving to avoid him the chauffeur decreased his speed, drove straight at him, knocked him down and drove on without stopping. The inference drawn from the chauffeur was that drunkenness had to be discouraged—at any price. The only visible night-workers we had seen were women road sweepers of uncertain ages with enormous brooms, dressed in faded blue denim boiler suits and indeterminate pieces of outer clothing to protect them from the cold. The roadways are magnificent with three lanes of traffic on either side; very few cars, but frequent trams. We had started with moderately low voices but this was soon forgotten. I told him how miserable and lonely I was up in my solitary room and he said how damned grateful he was for having Joan with him. We relived the extraordinary experience of the *Othello* reception and agreed that, if there was some means of communication other than grinning and gesticulating like a village idiot, we would discover they were all lovely people. 'Except the key lady on this floor,' said Larry, 'I can't get one hint of a smile out of her—the frosty bitch—but I will before we leave!' Vain boast, because he never did.

After the show Felix and Barry brazenly came up to my room bringing their own tin mugs for coffee and brandy and waited to phone their notices. We speculated idly on the geography of the missing seven floors between mine, the seventeenth, and the listed twenty-fourth to which no passenger was taken and came to the conclusion that all the scrambling equipment must be housed there with dozens of de-coders trying to make out what the hell everyone was saying. Again there was a long delay to London and, after their calls, they guiltily stole back to their own room.

Thursday, the last of the three successive first nights, dawned, with a fresh drama: Neville Thompson, our production manager, had flown back to London just after the Company's arrival to return with last minute props and wigs for *Love For Love*. In the early hours of the morning he, together with Peter Wood, the play's director, landed at the airport where it was discovered Neville had omitted to fill in one portion of a complicated document enabling him to re-enter the country. Peter was safely in the hotel but Neville was impounded in a waiting room! With indignation everyone tried to pull strings to release him—all to no avail. It was permitted to speak to him on the telephone or talk to him through a wire fence at the airport but, until bureaucracy had been satisfied, he was well and truly stuck. (Oddly enough the vital properties he had brought with him and his hand luggage were allowed through.)

The play was to have a full dress rehearsal during the day and, because Larry was in it, there was great press interest—so I stayed in my room. Late lunch time we all gathered in the restaurant; still no hope of Neville's release and the weather was very cold. We simply couldn't believe that a man could be held because he had forgotten to fill in one silly little line, equally that no one, apparently, had enough authority to set him free. George Rowbottom told us one of his grievances was that he couldn't shave but eventually an airport official lent him a razor. Heaven knew how he was faring for food in a waiting room considering we weren't exactly eating off the fat of the land in our £10 per diem hotel. But there were so many other problems connected with the opening that Neville tended to fade into the background. Not least of these was the translation of the play; as with *Hobson's Choice* Nina was to interpret each speech from the box just after it had been said. This was a fairly hit-or-miss solution even with a comedy containing visual humour but with a Restoration classic relying on period witticisms it sounded virtually impossible. It had earlier been suggested that we should supply a précis version of the text to accompany the programme but this was vetoed. The main set, designed by Lila de Nobili, was based on an original area of London near Covent Garden and was nearly as solid; there were innumerable costumes, an orchestra and a cast of forty giving the première of a seventeenth century play in a country which had never heard of Congreve and had no way of understanding it. This in itself was not so much a challenge as an act of total lunacy. However, we had made the gesture of opening one of our new productions in the USSR and we were hoisted on our own petard with the curtain shortly due to rise on this curious occasion.

Six of us, including Billie Whitelaw, who was playing Desdemona in *Othello*, and Maggie, in *Hobson*, but not in the cast of *Love For Love*, took one of the buses to the theatre having bought ourselves jars of nourishing caviar for the journey. These Felix adroitly opened for us with the aid of a rouble. The theatre was packed with earnest artisans in smocks and jeans with their ladies in cotton dresses and scarves tied round their heads, all eager to digest culture in large gulps. Perhaps not quite the ideal audience for the elegant Mr. Congreve, but dead keen. Also, as the play progressed, dead quiet. Heaven alone knows what dear little Nina, demurely dressed in black perched in her box with microphone in hand, made of such lines as 'To loggerheads they went, sir, and then he let fly at her a shot 'twixt wind and water, that won this fair maid's heart'! Anyway, however she translated the dialogue it must have been without a vestige of humour because one could have heard a pin drop in the packed theatre throughout most of the evening. This had a curious effect on the actors who had rehearsed their timing meticulously and were now over-acting to an alarming degree to try and squeeze some reaction from the spectators. Larry himself seemed to come off best because he had a marvellous piece of comic mime when, with wig awry and breeches adrift, he climbed out of a young girl's window, slid down the roof, balanced precariously on a narrow wall and, crossing himself with eyes closed, leapt over a wide gap before reaching the ground. This brought storms of applause and sudden realisation that it was a 'funny piece' which helped to liven up the second half of the evening.

The reception was enthusiastic, repeating the pattern of *Othello* with the audience storming round the stage. Back in the dressing-room I congratulated Larry and said it was a triumph. He smiled wryly. 'Yes, Ginny darling, a triumph— for the stage hands!' He then announced we should all hurry back because he was going to give a little party for 'us' to celebrate the three openings.

On all the tables there was scotch, gin, brandy—part of the Duty Free raid at London airport—and bottles of Russian wine. Instead of the set menu he had arranged that anyone could order from the à la carte. With an end of term abandon everyone was very gay—even the rather grim staff were wreathed in smiles. Finally Larry made an irreverent speech in which he sent up the Russians, their bumbling officialdom, their inefficient stage-hands; praised the interpreters (who were present!) and the English press for their moral support; ending with a toast 'To absent friends: poor Neville on his airport bench and Barry Norman who always seems to miss his dinner—when *does* he eat?' (He was, of course, upstairs wrestling with his London telephone call.) He invited Felix, Jack Lambert and myself up to his suite for a final drink. When we got up there Felix anxiously whispered that we shouldn't stay long as it was against the rules, to which Larry answered 'To hell with the rules! What do they think I want —to rape the lot of you?'

For better or worse the plays were on and Felix and Barry insisted I should take a morning off and do a little sight-seeing. On arrival at the hotel I had cashed a traveller's cheque in the orthodox fashion at the bureau. Sadly I'd looked at the small handful of coins I had exchanged for my ten English pounds—mainly to be expended on postcards and stamps—and made mental note to exercise husbandry in the future. But with careless abandon, knowing I was going shopping, I prepared to fling my money away. Alas, the bureau was unwomaned. However across the foyer, in a narrow corridor, there were some showcases with souvenirs. I went over and waved a traveller's cheque between the cases and a girl 'cashier' sitting behind something resembling a functional barricade. She squeaked 'Da' so I turned round and chose a primitive amber and silver necklace which seemed to cost a roubledom. I gave it to the lady with a five-pound cheque. There was an immediate reaction: she hurled herself onto her abacus and, with a deafening din, started to translate the day's sterling market onto her wires. The transaction was accompanied by a high-pitched running commentary from her as she bashed the abacus. (There are no cash registers in Moscow; all additions are made on abaci which gave a background effect of myriads of grasshoppers rubbing their legs together.) With a final yell of triumph she presented me with a fistful of notes: pounds, dollars, deutsch-marks, yens and you-name-thems. Thereafter I solemnly patronised her 'boutique' and came home with enough foreign currency to set up my own bureau de change—and more money than I had taken out with me!

On the shopping expedition we went to the famous 'Gum'

store (Gossudanstvienzy Universalny Magasin) which was a revelation. It is a series of tiny shops contained within a long, narrow building with an ornamental fountain in the centre; there are two floors with the upper one connected by Italianate iron bridges. The architecture fascinated us and Felix had with him a book he had bought in London giving its history. It had originally been built in its present state in 1888 although stone stores had stood on the site in the Middle Ages. The fountain had had a two-fold use: in the winter it served as a giant brazier to warm the ladies before making their purchases and, conversely, cooled them in the summer. The small booths housed the merchants who specialised in all luxury commodities. It was reminiscent of a more elegant Burlington Arcade having become a super-market. We were enthralled by it and said so to the inter-preter who accompanied us. He was delighted and told us it had been built for a long time to which we agreed. But Felix, quoting from his book, told him it had only been a 'department store' since 1953. This the youth—in his twenties —vehemently denied, although shown the text, and main-tained that the book was Western propaganda biased against the Soviet history. Vainly we tried to point out that there had been a way of life prior to the revolution but no argument would convince him. Although there were dozens of boutiques there was nothing to buy of any interest, either for practical purposes or as souvenirs. I challenged the inter-preter and said I would like to purchase a dress; he accepted this and conducted us to a corner emporium on the upper floor which had a few racks of shoddy cotton clothes—mostly made in other Communist countries—all highly priced. Through the boy I asked the shop owner if she had any cocktail dresses with inner conviction they would not be forthcoming. Certainly, was the answer, she had a large range but, unfortunately, they were all on display downstairs for a special fashion show. Could I see them? Certainly, but, unfortunately, the exhibition was closed at that moment. When would it be open? Unfortunately, again, she could not give me the exact time! It was a splendid example of the wearisome lengths to which the Russians go in order to save face. I had chosen purposely a cocktail dress because, throughout the six days I had not seen anybody wearing one, including the Minister of Culture, Madame Furtseva. How much simpler it would have been to have told me they were not worn in Moscow. Close to the dress shop was one which sold work made by goldsmiths in a small village in Moravia. There were goblets, flagons and cigarette boxes of heavy gold with three or four depths of enamel painted on top. They were very lovely and very expensive—the cheapest goblets starting at £65. We speculated on the customers and the interpreter assured us that they were quite ordinary and all the workers bought them . . . maybe, maybe.

We next went to the Armoury—opposite Gum in Red Square. I was not enthusiastic about this; guns are guns and bore me rigid but I didn't want to spoil the chaps' fun. There was a queue four deep stretching along the square but the interpreter took us straight to the head, muttered to the custodian and led us along corridors into a vast hall filled with brightly lit showcases reflecting shafts of light from thousands of diamonds which nearly blinded us. Here were the treasures of the Imperial Russian Monarchy; the coronation thrones, each more magnificent than the last, and all encrusted with precious stones; a procession of the various coronation and state coaches; hundreds of objets d'art by Fabergé; gold plate, crowns, sceptres, ikons, jewellery. In the centre showcases of this Aladdin's cave were the ceremonial robes and private clothes of the Czars and the court. One was outstanding in the midst of this dazzling magnificence: the wedding dress of 'Little Catharine'; it was ground length, made of solid silver thread, of elegant simplicity and without adornment. She was obviously very short—no more than five foot—with a figure that would have been the envy of any present day vital-statistician. All the clothes were in pristine condition including the underwear and night attire. The three of us were speechless with wonder and surprise and all round us were Muscovites experiencing the same emotions. They were being herded into large groups and given lectures on what we assumed was their past history. Although not one of them possessed any jewellery they viewed the treasures with appreciation and no apparent envy. Having spent some hours there we left reluctantly, promising ourselves to return.

That evening the critics, Jack Lambert of the *Sunday Times*, Felix Barker of the *Evening News*, Barry Norman of the *Daily Mail* and Maureen Cleave of the *Evening Standard*, asked me to dine with them in the main restaurant as their guest. This was quite a gesture, because, unlike us, they all had tickets for their meals which had to be accounted for. Somebody—obviously Barry—had missed a dinner and after some heated argument from the waiter I was allowed to eat with them. Felix was returning to London, Jack and Maureen were going to Leningrad for a couple of days, Barry was staying for the remainder of our visit and this was a celebration evening. When the Company had finished their supper one of the chaperoned kids, Leonard Whiting, swept past us and said 'We're all going downstairs, there's a super night-club.' It had to take a fourteen-year-old to discover that. He was right in one respect: it was a night-club in as much as one could buy a drink and dance to an ill-defined noise. Larry and Joan joined us and the critics gave them copies of the first English reports of our success. Larry was absolutely thrilled because till then he had only had scantily translated versions of the Russian papers. We talked about the packed houses and Barry asked why one particularly large box—it could accommodate fifteen to twenty people—had permanently remained empty although it could have been sold at every performance. Larry replied that, to the best of his knowledge, it was reserved for the Soviet Government and could not be sold to the public. We agreed it seemed undemocratic not to put it to use and impolite, if not impolitic, that it had not been occupied by any of the government heads at the first nights.

I received a chaming farewell present from Jack with this accompanying note: 'To the National Theatre Company. I don't know how you tolerate the physical presence of critics, but you have done so most nobly. Though well aware that you have oceans of the stuff already, I shall think myself privileged if you will accept these two bottles of whisky, which will surely come in useful somehow. With them comes every possible good wish for the rest of the tour—but don't forget we shall be needing you back in London. Regardless of what I may have written and may yet write, please accept my respect and admiration, you fine old load of mummers. Jack Lambert.'

It was with mutual regret that they left us. This experiment of press and actors sharing the same experiences had taught both sides to see and appreciate each other's problems in a way that would have been impossible in England.

The Soviet State Circus was scheduled to open within a few days and an invitation was issued to a number of us to attend the school itself and watch a demonstration. The Circus School is quite unique. There are approximately three thousand applicants each year with vacancies for only ninety pupils. The training starts at eleven years old and lasts for a ten year period; during this time the pupils have to attain the highest proficiency in every aspect of circus life: juggling, clowning, miming, trapeze acrobatics, stunt aerobatics, animal handling, ballet and tumbling. When they receive their diplomas they are fully capable of taking any part in any of the State Circuses throughout the Union. The competition to enter the school is high and the honour to become a pupil is possibly only second to becoming an astronaut. Not only do the children learn their profession but they have to attend academic classes and gain a university degree. The demonstration was focused on a younger graduate who was shortly to make his début at the Moscow State Circus: he was a superb all-rounder and excelled as a mimecomic which our actors were quick to appreciate. Among the audience was Konni Zilliacus, convalescing after treatment in a Black Sea sanatorium, who was an ardent circus fan and an old friend of Alexandr Voloshin, the Director. I had a glass of the ubiquitous Coca-Cola with Alexandr Voloshin and was made a life member of the State Circus, an honour only accorded once previously to a non-acting person. He invited me to bring Larry to a private dress rehearsal of the circus proper in two days' time. Unfortunately it coincided with an *Othello* night so Larry was unable to attend but two of the Company accepted the invitation.

On the appointed day I awoke feeling ill and feverish but determined to see the rehearsal. We arrived at the theatre stage-door but were firmly barred from entry until I remembered my membership badge pinned under my coat collar. Feeling like an old Western sheriff and slightly foolish, I turned back my collar and flashed the badge. It worked like a charm—smiles and open sesame. With ill-concealed smugness my chums and I were escorted like royalty into the auditorium and ushered into the third row immediately behind M. Voloshin and his wife. To our surprise the interior is tiny and intimate, unlike our circuses. Also the 'ring' is more horseshoe-shaped with the orchestra seated above the one large entrance at the top of the horseshoe. There were a mere handful of spectators and we felt very grateful for this privilege and the close proximity of our seats; this feeling lasted until the interval. To a stirring march from the orchestra well-drilled circus hands swiftly erected high steel bars round the ring with some stools, a swing and a seesaw inside it. The music stopped, the barred entrance opened and twelve hefty tigers disdainfully strolled in followed by a tiny blonde carrying a small whip. The exit was closed leaving her in the centre of a veritable lions' den. Looking pretty sulky the tigers selected their stools and sat down. At a word of command from the girl one padded over and sat on the seesaw, she called to another who refused to budge; she repeated the command more tersely and was answered by a deep growl. Again she spoke to it but the growls were taken up by the others who were getting generally restless and fidgety. Although she still appeared to be calm, we certainly weren't. The growls soon developed into roars and—in a second's flash—one of the animals leapt at another and started fighting. That was the signal for two things to happen simultaneously: all the animals fought together and, from nowhere it seemed, the outer cage was surrounded by attendants carrying long iron poles with pronged ends and hose pipes which they immediately used on the animals, guiding them through the exit which had been hastily opened. This was done without any panic or alarm but I couldn't help feeling that the amount of adrenalin that I personally was exuding might have further incensed the beasts. I was exonerated at the brief inquest held after their withdrawal. None of us had spotted that they were tigers and

144

tigresses, and one of the ladies was shortly coming into season! Some ten minutes later the girl reappeared with her charges, calm and unruffled. The only outward difference was that her whip had been replaced with a more formidable looking bar that she used as a premonitory threat and the act went through without further incident. At the end I discovered I was shaking and sweating with fever and fright and suggested I went home. The Circus Director's wife who spoke a little French was horrified at this idea. Had I got a doctor? No, I said. Right, come with me; you are a member of our organisation and we will deal with you! There was nothing for it but to follow her with even more trepidation behind the scenes. As we made our way past acrobats, tumblers and four unchained bears, thoughts were chasing through my muddled head: I remembered horses were given pills by blowing them through a pipe down their throat and thermometers were put in invidious parts of dogs' anatomy. These speculations were brought to a halt when Madame Voloshina opened a door and we walked into a room with a dozen naked men showering themselves. I smiled weakly and bowed to them as we passed. She then knocked on a door which was opened by a genial man in a white coat—the vet— and we entered the most modern surgery I've ever seen. Next door was a fully-equipped operating theatre. Some rapid sentences were exchanged, a Russian-English phrase book, printed in the Boer War, was thrust into my hand and she left. Casting my eye over a list of sufferings ranging from Bubonic plague (suspected) to emergency childbirth, I threw myself into an alarming display of dumbshow indicating my symptoms. He must have understood because, having counted my pulse and popped a thermometer—into my mouth—he opened an enormous refrigerator from which he gave me two injections, some pills and a glass of evil-tasting medicine.

145

He mimed that I shouldn't eat but go to bed at once. We shook hands and I walked back the way I had come, musing on the contradictions between the efficiency I had just witnessed and the backwardness of much of the Soviet way of life. My hosts sent me home by car making me promise that if any of our Company were taken ill the Circus doctor should be sent for. For the record the treatment worked.

Next evening Barry and I joined Larry in his room. He told us that he had lunched with some government officials who had been so carried away by his performance that they asked him what he would most like to do during his visit. Taking them literally he replied that he would like to meet Kruschev. There was an instant silence followed by yet another face-saving excuse. He was too ill, he could not have visitors, etc. We loudly and freely discussed the obstacles we had encountered since our arrival and came to the conclusion that this was a reign of total fear. Rumours were flying high that Kosygin was on the way out and we speculated on whether Kruschev was in fact still alive. This led to Larry again commenting on the empty State box. We all became so insular and outraged over this snub that Barry said he would straight away ring his paper. That was his intention, but he was not given a connection that night. He rejoined us and said that the exchange had told him no calls were being put through until the morrow. Larry was wild with rage and, at the top of his not inconsiderable voice, let forth the loudest flow of invective punctuated with Kenneth Tynan's four-letter television word. In spite of the receptive audiences it was clear that he wanted to get home. The pressure was beginning to tell on everyone; the initial impetus which made the three openings possible had faded, leaving everybody physically and mentally exhausted. The National Theatre had been in existence for less than two years and the superhuman effort put into this first foreign tour was taxing everyone's stamina. A number of our staff had already gone back; Barry—to my regret—was also leaving; but Ken Tynan and Albert Finney were coming out for a couple of nights, which was something to look forward to!

In the meantime I helped Douglas Warth with his film for Pathé; Larry and Joan looked splendid with the sentinels in Red Square, Billie Whitelaw braved the hydrofoil on the river Mosba; and I was persuaded to meet him at a children's theatre in the suburbs of Moscow. I showed the taxi driver the written address and sat beside him. After a while we started talking, neither understanding one word the other said, but it passed the time amiably. He dropped me outside a church hall swarming with mothers and children. Inside I found Douglas waiting for the run-through to start. The theatre is aimed for very young children. The plots are simple (this one being the adventure of a spaceman) the only difference between it and the Western equivalent being that all the actors are animals! There was a silver fox, a racoon, a monkey, a cat that allowed white mice to play all over its body, a six-foot brown bear bespectacled and capped who manned the craft and, for light relief, a trio of penguins who would make the Beatles look to their laurels. The commentator was a raddled mynah bird who gave a fluent Russian running commentary. The performance lasted for twenty never-to-be-forgotten minutes with perfect ensemble playing from the cast. This extraordinary set-up is run by a man and wife as an extension of their animal hospital—much like our P.D.S.A. The youngsters bring their pets for treatment and help to train them for the stage to encourage the children eventually to appreciate live theatre.

I dined at the Press club with Anya and a man I'd met at the Soviet Embassy in London who was now a government cultural aide. I told them that Larry was thrilled by the audience's reaction to the plays but also slightly hurt by the governmental cold shoulder—not personally but for the Company's sake—and reminded them that we were on an Anglo-Russo Cultural visit. They escorted me back by tram and I was amused that the conductress had run out of tickets, so gave us old ones from the floor. Two days later Larry received an invitation from the Soviet Ministry asking him and the Company to an official luncheon at the Palace of Congress. The ballerina Galina Ulanova acted as one of the interpreters. This, I am convinced, would have been issued automatically but perhaps with their own internal troubles they had forgotten their party manners. Moreover, on the last night of *Othello*, the box was filled with Soviet ministers headed by the current President, Mr. Mikoyan, who received Larry and presented him with a cask of brandy grown from his own vineyards in Armenia. National honour was satisfied. I sped back to the telephone with a mission to spread the good news from Aix to Ghent and, at two-thirty, contacted the British press with the story of our final triumph.

The plane-call for Berlin was listed for the unlikely hour of four o'clock in the morning to Copenhagen; from there to Frankfürt and, at long last, Berlin early afternoon. All this to avoid flying over East Berlin which would have taken a few hours! How stupid can humans get? Bleary-eyed and loaded with odd loot, we piled into the Russian plane on the first leg of the journey. At Copenhagen airport we suddenly realised we were in a free country—it was a strange feeling. There was an hour's wait and, when the flight was called, some of the Company were missing, including Larry. Further confusion arose when they arrived because it was a scheduled flight with added passengers and there weren't enough seats. Larry immediately said he would take a later plane but this was overruled.

The Company were staying in three different hotels and the first thing that struck us was the overpowering luxury of the Kempinski compared with the Ukraine in Moscow. Service of almost any kind could be had by pressing one of twelve bells in bathroom or bedroom—heaven. We inspected the theatre, one of many built in Berlin just after the war at the cost of several million pounds. Although delighted by it, it reminded Larry of the procrastinated National Theatre of Great Britain and he spat out a few pithy comments on parsimony.

Othello opened the following night and was received with the same tumultuous applause as in Russia. There were a number of English in the audience who hadn't been able to get seats for it at the Old Vic and had flown over for the night. We were playing *Othello* and *Love For Love* for the week's stay in Berlin, which put heavy exertion on poor Larry as he was in every performance, plus certain official functions that could not be avoided.

Next day he stayed in bed until the evening and Joan and Billie Whitelaw came to my room. We all three decided to laze about in dressing-gowns—I think this was a reaction after the nervous strain of Moscow. As one of the parting presents I had been given four pounds of delectable caviar normally reserved for the Government and not on sale in the shops; this had travelled in paper and tinfoil in the refrigerators of the different planes and then lodged in the hotel fridge. We ordered some champagne and the caviar and ate it all. Pity, really, I'd always adored it—now I loathe it.

Berlin struck us as a very odd place—one was aware of wealth and the bustle of apparent activity with very little to show for it. God knows it was bombed, but even now those famous names like Kurfürstendamm and Unter den Linden are long streets with large gaps, many half-blitzed buildings and a few new ones mostly built by the Americans. The people have an uneasy air about them probably due to the pervasiveness of that blasted wall which snakes its way through the capital. It is not very high, topped with masses of barbed wire, grey-green in colour; there are occasional openings literally stuffed with coiled barbed wire making it impossible to see through. Everybody we met was anxious that we should enjoy our stay, the plays were a fantastic success—on the last night of *Othello* the applause lasted for thirty-five minutes—but still we were all eager to get home. I telephoned the office and asked my secretary to alert the press and television of our arrival and warned Larry I had done so. At London Airport I was determined to get customs through with him as quickly as possible and, when asked if I had anything to declare I answered 'Gratitude to be in England—and a few memories from Russia!' They allowed me through to muster the press into a reception committee and I returned for Larry. He had got a mixed bag of trophies all carefully listed. Leaving Joan to cope with them we emerged into the arrival lounge and the familiar cameras and questions. We really *were* home.

6

The Aftermath of the Tour

That same day I flew to Africa for a quick holiday and returned the day before the London first night of *Love For
Love*. While away I hadn't felt well but put it down to
fatigue from the tour. In the office, the opening day, I
secretly took my temperature and discovered it was 103—
which seemed a little high. That night I welcomed the press
and played hostess to them in the interval in a hazy stupor;
then went straight home. Next morning my doctor gaily said
both my lungs had packed up and I had double pneumonia.
I called Larry and told him. His immediate reaction was
'God, how long will you be away?' followed by a belated
'I'm so sorry for you, darling.' The doctor's original airy
estimate of 'about two weeks' stretched to six; and I returned
shortly before Christmas which we spent with Larry and
Joan at Brighton. A number of friends came in for drinks
on Christmas morning and, after a late luncheon, he and I
volunteered to do the washing-up—the staff had been given
the day off and the other guests retired to bed. Both arrayed
in bright-coloured folksy aprons we tossed for choice; wash-
ing or drying? I won the latter. Faced with a hugger-mugger
stack of dirty glasses, plates, cutlery and saucepans my
friend proceeded methodically to direct the utensils and, of

course, me. We had a sly nip to help us through and finished triumphantly without one casualty.

In the New Year it became obvious that the proposed season's programme was going to be the usual tough one. At least four new productions; a spring tour; a long season at the Queen's Theatre (in place of Chichester) to run concurrently with the Old Vic, followed immediately by a protracted autumn tour. The first new play was *A Flea In Her Ear*, a Georges Feydeau farce brilliantly translated by John Mortimer. Jacques Charon from the Comédie Française was to direct it. He was fun, gay, amusing and wonderful to work with. From the commencement—in the rehearsal room attached to the offices—there was a feeling of gaiety and relaxation; rare and very welcome. It was an instantaneous success; possibly the biggest compliment given to the Company came from M. Feydeau's brother at the party after the first night. He does not speak or understand any English and, with astonishment, told me he simply couldn't believe that he had not just seen a play in French. I was very sad when Jacques left, taking with him his Gallic ebullience.

It was scheduled to present John Osborne's adaptation of Lope de Vega's classic *La Fianza Satisfecha* after *Flea*. This play was one of the very first to have been announced for presentation at the original press conference in 1963, but, for unknown reasons, it had been postponed. Larry sent for me and asked my private reaction to the possibility of John Dexter's leaving the National. I had to tell him the truth, which was that he and I were antipathetic to each other; he bullied me, ridiculed me and always made me feel inadequate. I said I thought he was one of the best directors, to which Larry agreed, but I added I didn't care for his open criticism of Larry and the National. I explained that this was my personal opinion which might be biased because he didn't like me. He told me the Osborne play would be post-poned yet again and his own production of O'Casey's *Juno and the Paycock* would take first place. It was essential to have eight productions running by August; four at the Vic and four at the Queen's Theatre. It was finally settled that the Osborne play, entitled *A Bond Honoured*, directed by John Dexter, would open at the beginning of June. As was customary I asked John Osborne into my office for a drink and a chat about the publicity for the play, and—although I already knew the answer—his attitude toward interviews. It wasn't difficult to be proved right; his reply was 'My dear girl, for God's sake *nothing*.' This exercise was simple; he had recently moved to a new ex-directory number which placed him out of reach.

A Bond Honoured was a one-act play which accompanied *Black Comedy*. In the interval it struck me that the press weren't too enthusiastic for it which was borne out by their notices next morning. The day following I arrived in the office shortly before ten o'clock and the three telephones were ringing as I walked in. Answering them as best I could I gathered that John, without pre-warning, had sent personal telegrams to each individual critic rounding on them for slating the play. They, in turn, were cross as two ticks and were all demanding his number which I refused to disclose. Later in the morning John himself rang me: 'Darling, have you had a beastly time?' 'Yes, thanks,' I replied, 'absolutely foul.' He then apologised profusely for not telling me his intentions and said he was quite prepared to stand by his own action and would talk to any of them on the telephone. Although this let-out was a relief I assured him I could keep on stalling because I felt, in his present mood he would probably make the situation worse. Next morning this was justified; the various journalists had sharpened their pens and gone to town. John appeared on television and gave a number of acid interviews. After a few days of this bally-hooing he suddenly said to me 'Virginia, I've been very silly and I don't want to go on with it—please tell them.' I roared with laughter and told him I had no intention of repeating that; the best thing would be to let it die a natural death. I thought how deliciously stupid he is because he's nothing like the public image he builds up for himself. I'm sure the motive behind that little performance was for a joke.

The eight productions were now in the repertoire and it was decided to give the Company their holiday in July before the concurrent seasons commenced in August. One evening, during the vacation period, I asked my secretary to go up the corridor to see if the late editions had been delivered. My next recollection was lying flat on my back with a man in a white coat peering over me saying 'You've dislocated your shoulder and we're going to give you a general anaesthetic.' Playing for time, not knowing where the hell I was, I asked him to repeat that. He said it— slowly—which gave me a chance to find some sort of answer: it came, pat; I told him I'd just had a large meal! (Which meant I couldn't have any anaesthetic with safety.) I didn't know it then but it was close on ten o'clock—I'd been out cold for four hours. I'd apparently blacked-out and fallen between my heavy 'executive', according to the catalogue, chair and the desk, hence the shoulder. He asked me if I had had a similar experience before; I shook my head, which hurt my shoulder, I sat up, raised my arm, there was an almighty click and a nasty pain but the shoulder was back without the dreaded anaesthetic. A sister 'took my particulars' including asking my religion. I told her I was an agnostic to which she replied 'That's bloody brave of you.' I thought it was bloody impertinent of *her*, but didn't say so. I was wheeled off and during the next fortnight given twenty-two different tests, each nastier than the last including a spiffing lumbar puncture. All of these proved negative physically but positive mentally—I had a full-scale nervous breakdown and was sent to stay with friends in Chichester who nursed me, in a cottage without a telephone and no theatre distractions.

After some weeks of this therapeutic treatment I was sent off to Tangier for a three week holiday. I returned mentally stronger, but weighing only six stone ten, shortly before the opening of *The Storm*—a turgid Russian classic. Greeted effusively by my colleagues and delighted to be back I settled down to work. Within a fortnight I had lost three more pounds. Dear Kenneth Rae had a strict talk to me and insisted, on behalf of the Board, that I went back to Africa to relax and not show my face in the offices until I was completely fit.

7

The Last Act

WHEN I returned to England in December I had a long private talk with Larry. He was very concerned about my health and wanted to make sure that the pressure of the job wouldn't cause me to have another breakdown; wholeheartedly I echoed his sentiments! He asked me if I had given any thought towards an alternative while I had been away. I told him I had vaguely considered approaching the Moroccan Embassy to discover if they would consider me for their English publicist as I was familiar with and loved the country. We agreed anyway that I should put this idea into action. I then specifically asked him if he would prefer me not to return to the National. His answer was a vehement negative; followed by assurances that his only consideration was for my well-being. We parted with a mutual arrangement that we would give it a three-month trial; if, at the end of that period, either of us felt it wasn't working out we would call it a day. I later had an audience with the Ambassadress, Her Royal Highness the Princess Lalla Aicha, who told me that all such appointments were handled by the government in Rabat—which seemed a long way to go for an interview!

My first 'public appearance' was at an annual New Year party Kenneth Rae gave in the offices. Ken Tynan and I were discussing specious plans for the future when he suddenly said, 'If they don't do the Hochhuth play I shall hand in my resignation.' I paid little heed to the remark, he had made similar threats in the past, and I knew nothing about the Hochhuth play. Unfortunately that blissful state didn't last long. Ken went to Rome in mid-January to tape an interview with Richard Burton. While there he talked to Burton about the possibility of him playing Winston Churchill in *Soldiers* by Rolf Hochhuth. In the uncanny way gossip has of getting itself transmuted into newsprint it appeared in an Italian paper and was picked up by an English one. This categorically stated that Richard Burton would be seen as Churchill in *'The' Soldiers* at the Old Vic. Faced with this bald statement I hied up the corridor for confirmation or denial; neither of which I got. I was given to understand that the script, which was sub rosa, would be a matter for the Board on account of its controversial subject. Swearing an oath of secrecy I was allowed to take it home and read it. Ignoring the merits or demerits of the play, I was at once struck by the impossibility of producing it while the censor's office was still in existence. There were valid reasons for withholding a licence. Primarily, a number of descendants of the characters concerned were still alive and their permission would have to be obtained. Also, in the version I read, there was a scene in Churchill's room when the actor impersonating Sir Winston is, supposedly, in his bath and enters stark naked except for a towel thrown over one shoulder. Female nudes are not allowed to move on the stage so, presumably, the ruling would apply to a male. This point really was only a personal quibble because I couldn't convince myself that a serious actor would consent to act with his private parts exposed. But an integral section of the play, suggesting that Churchill deliberately planned

General Sikorski's death, appeared to me a substantial argument in the Censor's favour. An author is granted poetic licence when dealing with purely fictitious characters but it is against the law in England to make serious allegations against real people without any substantiation. On September 29th 1968 the Lord Chamberlain's jurisdiction as Censor ceased to exist. I came to the conclusion that the only way to circumvent the Lord Chamberlain would be to present the play to Club Members. This, I thought, would be utterly impossible. How could the National Theatre of Great Britain be turned into a Theatre Club for certain performances? The ensuing chaos with the booking public, the inevitable storm of abuse from the general public would make us such a laughing stock that it wouldn't be worth presenting the play—even though it prove a masterpiece.

Armed with my own opinions and all five volumes of the script, together totalling six-and-a-half-hours-worth of play and reading time, I went to the office and gave my humble report. Although in complete agreement with me in principle, I was asked not to say this to the press nor, indeed divulge to anyone that I had read it. On the other hand it was obliquely implied that I should keep a watching ear on Ken's activities. I was also given to understand that it would become a major Board issue within the next few weeks or until such time as Herr Hochhuth had completed the script and made certain emendations to it. Larry wasn't present at this meeting; he was deep in rehearsals for his next production *The Dance of Death*.

I returned to my office feeling like a poor man's Mata Hari and praying it would prove a storm in a teacup. For a few days everything was peaceful; I countered the sporadic press enquiries with harmless dismissive answers; but I had reckoned without Ken. Ever a champion of a good lost cause, he fairly hurled himself into this one. Going out on his own limbo he assiduously applied himself to the task of ridding England from the maws of the archaic and near-obsolete Lord Chamberlain. With all the bite, wit and pith at his not inconsiderable command he wrote brilliant derogatory articles for various magazines and newspapers; rallied his most influential friends, left and right; offered himself as a speaker at meetings; wrote endless impassioned letters; made endless long-distance calls—all directed toward the end of censorship in its present form. Never has any author been so championed by a critic. Unhappily, in his single-mindedness he tended to forget the harm he might do to others, unintentionally, because he is not in any way an unkind man. His beliefs and ideals blur reality as when, two years earlier, he publicly stated he was in favour of sexual intercourse on the stage. I reminded him that David had publicised *Hamlet*, when Ken appeared as the Player King, and I challenged him, as an actor, to prove that he would be able to 'perform' on cue, six times a week, plus two matinées. He said he was sure he could, but he had given up acting.

In the next few weeks life became increasingly difficult down my end of the corridor. Ken was fighting tooth and nail for something in which he passionately believed: freedom of speech and action and an over-all desire to be free of Establishment, in any shape. The lone wolf and his indivi-dualness came uppermost, which was in direct conflict with my own strict discipline in the theatre. I had been brought up to show loyalty to the management employing me—in this case the Board and Larry—or, if I didn't like it, to leave. Conversely, Ken's brilliant critical career in latter years of necessity made him a soloist and a non-conformist. Both viewpoints are perfectly valid but bound to cause disharmony when yoked together. I was sweating blood to under-play *Soldiers* while Ken was exerting every effort to blow it up. Larry, at this juncture, was concentrating on the mammoth part of Edgar and I had few opportunities of discussing the problem in depth with him. I had been given the broad policy line and I adhered to it.

After the opening night of *The Dance of Death*, in which Larry gave one of the most moving and profound performances of his life, he appeared in the office more often. The decisive board meeting had to be postponed and was contingent on two things: Herr Hochhuth's final translated amended script and Larry's availability—he was scheduled to appear in the provinces during the spring tour. Eventually a date in April was fixed. Rolf Hochhuth came to England for a few days and, rather to my amazement, I learnt that he couldn't speak English. Why should I be surprised; Ken doesn't speak German, but art is international.

A diversion from *Soldiers* came when John Dexter arrived back from America, where he had been for many weeks directing a play. One evening Joan asked if she could borrow my office and use my ex-directory line in order to speak to him privately. A few days later Larry asked to see me. He told me that John would be leaving us; and we prepared a brief statement which said that the National had agreed to release him as an Associate Director in order for him to expand his activities. It was hoped he would direct certain productions at the Old Vic in the future. This announcement was nullified a few days later by John himself when he gave an interview in which he stated he had been fired. The reason for this caused a few days' idle speculation privately; and the fact that the National was now lacking its original Associate Directors, leaving Larry without his two aides, was mentioned briefly in print.

13a

13b

14

15a

15b

16a

16b

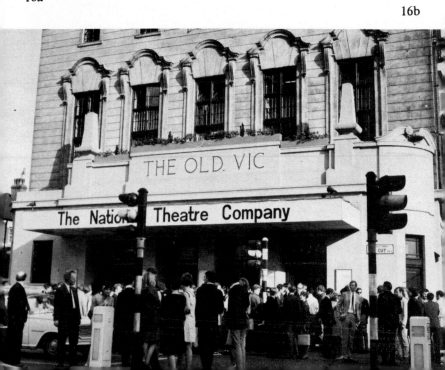

But it was only a short respite. With a few more weeks to go until the decisive meeting the office tension heightened. Odd rumours of heads rolling were whispered and minor anarchy stalked the corridor. Press interest was stirred in the National Theatre Charter and its terms of office. It was noted that certain board members had resigned. (One had for domestic reasons; the other having done so months previously without comment at the time, but this was now updated.) The translated copies of the script ultimately arrived with the author's proviso that it still was not the final version. The atmosphere was thoroughly unhealthy and the day of the meeting heavy with suspense: everyone seemed apprehensive; no one knew what the outcome would be. It was timed for the afternoon. Larry had been in the office since the morning; Ken arrived, jauntily whistling, at lunchtime; the Board individually. As the door closed I sat like someone waiting in a hospital for the verdict. I was given it in a short clinical paragraph: 'The Board of the National Theatre holds an option on a play by Herr Hochhuth entitled *Soldiers*. Sir Winston Churchill, Lord Cherwell, Lord Alanbrooke and Sir Arthur Harris were to be represented by actors on the stage. Some of the characters, in particular Sir Winston Churchill and Lord Cherwell, were grossly maligned and in consequence the Board unanimously considered that the play was unsuitable for production at the National Theatre. The Director expressed himself as being unhappy at this decision.' I knew these eighty words were dynamite—particularly the ten from Larry which were echoing his own regret that the author had not been given further time to complete his play. I started telephoning the press. Their reaction was predictable since this was hot news. I patiently explained that I had nothing further to add to the statement but this didn't stop my 'phones ringing with demands for details which

I wasn't in a position to give. On the other hand, very understandably in the circumstances, Ken was not so loth to expound to them.

The evening papers carried the story with added quotes from Ken. In one of them he said that Sir Laurence and he would both resign. This equivocal remark caused all the journalists working for morning papers to ring me like fluttering pigeons. I buzzed Larry in the office for his answer: It came: 'Don't be bloody silly, Ginny darling, I wouldn't dream of resigning.' Splendid, but impossible to give as a quote. All I could do was to maintain it was untrue, but the damage was done; it was in print—and even the press believe each other's papers.

At half-past nine I left the office mentally and physically exhausted. There was no let-up at home so I went out to dinner and, with cowardice, removed the receiver before going to bed. Next day the papers blazoned the story with quotes and comments from Ken and the Chairman, Lord Chandos, who had been forced to become the other protagonist. But this was only the start. Abiding by the author's plea that the play was unfinished and therefore shouldn't be made public, the controversy was mainly hypothetical. The only known facts that had been leaked out were that it concerned the bombing of Dresden, the characters were national figures and the English war leader hero was imputed of plotting the cold-blooded murder of one of his allies. Sufficient to whet the public's appetite but a large Harvest Festival carrot for the press, who bayed, cajoled and wooed me for a script. Telling, I hope convincingly, lie after lie, I held them off. They realised I was acting under orders, as I knew they were, and it was just part of our job. Fortunately Herr Hochhuth came to the rescue. He made a statement through a third party affirming that the irrefutable data proving Churchill to be responsible for a deliberate murder was lodged in a Societé Anonyme bank in Switzerland with instructions that it should not be opened for fifty years. This rather ingenuous red herring initiated a new line of argument and conjecture. The Czech pilot who flew the fatal plane which exploded after take-off—and the only known survivor—voluntarily swore the machine had not been sabotaged; as did members of the security guard who had been in Gibraltar at the time. Some of the left-wing papers accused Lord Chandos of partisanship since he had been one of Churchill's aides during the war. Ken publicly allied himself with Larry on this issue and many of his statements included proudly 'Sir Laurence and I'. Immersed in his subject, he anachronistically avowed in print that he planned to join the resistance. Lord Chandos accepted the challenge and volleyed back with a rejoinder which included a devastating comment on Ken's attitude. He said: ' . . . And I think it's very odd that Mr. Tynan should conduct a campaign against his chairman and board, while retaining his salary. Now I see he's "joined the resistance"—I suppose that means taking to the maquis while continuing to draw his pay. He's done good work for the theatre, of course, but he *will* take off like a guided missile.'

Heaven knows it was a battle all right with no apparent hope of cease-fire. In the vortex one man was silent: Larry. His only personal comment had been the few words issued with the original press statement. Recognising that the situation had got thoroughly out of hand he sent for Ken and had a private chat with him. Later I saw him and he told me Ken was hoping to present the play elsewhere; therefore any future enquiries would not concern the National Theatre. Next day the *Times* printed a brilliantly astringent letter from Larry which succinctly inferred 'this is the end of the affair'. With a sigh of relief I mentally classed *Soldiers* and Hochhuth as obscene language.

Larry's work schedule was a pretty tight one: he was appearing in *The Dance of Death* and *Love For Love*, both in London and on the provincial tour, also directing *Three Sisters* which was to open at the National in July. The Company were essaying their second foreign visit in the autumn, a protracted tour of Canada including the peak attraction at Expo '67 in Montreal. This entailed meticulous long-term rehearsal planning incorporating cast adjustments and replacements. The three plays chosen for Canada were *A Flea In Her Ear*, *Love For Love* and *Othello* with Larry in the last two. For good measure he had consented to fly over to Montreal for a weekend to make an opening speech at Expo' conjointly with his friend and fellow actor Jean-Louis Barrault. To confuse the obvious Larry proposed to speak in French and Barrault English!

Although the object of his visit was to promote British theatre in Canada, the press at London Airport were still sniffing after Hochhuth. He parried their leading questions with great skill and guided them back to Montreal.

While *Three Sisters* was in rehearsal I received an urgent summons to go to his office. He poured me a drink and baldly told me he was going to have some treatment for a growth in the next few weeks, adding that he was fairly sure it was cancer. Stunned beyond belief I sat and gazed at him. He looked so fit and well, and I simply couldn't grasp what he'd said. Jocularly telling me to pull myself together and for God's sake have another drink, he said he would know definitely within a few days, then immediately changed the subject. Alone, I prayed for it not to be true. The next week he again sent for me. The result of the tests was positive. In his original planning he had intended waiting until after

Three Sisters had opened before starting the treatment. Now, after consultation with his medical advisers, he had changed his mind. He had been given two alternatives: at this particular moment the disease had only just made itself manifest and, with one kind of treatment, it would be possible to arrest it or hold it at bay for a few weeks. On the other hand a different method had recently been experimented with that could eradicate the cancer if taken at this immediate juncture. Without hesitation Larry chose the latter believing that it would help the doctors and give them more chance to develop the never-ending research for a cure. The treatments were to be administered regularly twice a week for three weeks, and he had agreed to enter the hospital the next day. I asked him how he wanted me to deal with the press. Owing to an attack of laryngitis a couple of weeks earlier, he had to miss a performance which had passed without comment; should I endeavour to keep the news quiet? His unexpected reply was a vehement 'No!' On the contrary, he wanted it made public; rationally arguing that *one* performance might escape notice but not seven. Furthermore he wanted the nature of the disease to be made known, saying he thought it might give hope to others similarly afflicted 'if the guinea-pig pulls it off'. He was right, of course, the speculation and misconjectures would have been legion; but never have I admired anyone so much as I did him for his incredible courage. He gave me the precise medical terms, describing the illness and the treatment to be employed. Apart from confirming with one of his surgeon's that the words accurately described his condition, he treated the composition of the announcement with dispassion. While checking the spelling of some unaccustomed phrases I heard him arguing passionately about the future rehearsal schedule for *Three Sisters*. His idea was to have a treatment—which necessitated him resting for twenty-four hours after its completion—then return to the theatre to continue directing the play. No one, including Larry himself, had any notion of the affect of these sessions or what effect they might have on him; but in the face of such lion bravery nobody wished to deter him.

Of all the momentous press statements I had put out in my life this was the worst. Encouraged by a large brandy and Larry's own courage, I started telephoning the news round the world. Realistically, because of the time-lag and the proximity of the Canadian tour, I gave them priority. It was obvious that Larry would not be strong enough to play *Othello*. The English papers headlined the news, although some had misinterpreted the medical term indicating the exact nature of the illness.

Feeling fit and well Larry left the hospital the morning following his first treatment and went down to Brighton. It was a warm, sunny day and he went on to the beach. In the evening he felt ill and feverish and it was discovered he had a slight pneumonia. To everyone, putting him first, this seemed the last straw. He pretended to be furious with the hospital, joking that he had gone there to be cured of cancer, which he knew he had, only to be given pneumonia which he didn't want. Luckily it wasn't serious but it proved that he would have to pay some heed in the future. Joanie telephoned me and suggested she should give a small press conference to the specialist writers to allay any further public alarm. Inwardly congratulating her, I immediately put it in motion. At the end of rehearsing Masha in *Three Sisters* she came into the office looking very pretty in bright pink. She made it clear to the press from the outset that she was prepared to answer *any* question that they cared to ask her relating to Larry's illness. Later she told me she had done this without consulting Larry for fear he might have prevented her. In this she was quite right because she begged the help of the press to print that it was imperative for Larry to stay in the hospital until the treatment had been concluded. She was also right psychologically, because her frankness with them assuaged much of the alarm that the double illness had engendered. It was felt that the position couldn't be desperate if his own wife was so sanguine. She was taking her cue from Larry and matching him in moral courage. He, of course, was furious that he had been trapped and, immediately his temperature subsided, became impatient to start working again. The pneumonia had interrupted the treatment and upset the original schedule which would delay his return for a further week, but he discovered it was far easier to get into a hospital than it was, now, to get out—thanks to Joan! He had endless telephone conversations with his assistant producer, the stage manager, the production manager and the costume designer. The brilliant Czech designer Josef Svoboda had done the sets and was in permanent orbit between Europe and the United States. Contacting him by telephone round the globe occupied some of Larry's restless hours. At the end of the week he asked me to visit him. It was a treatment day and while I drank his champagne, he tried to explain to me what took place. He told me that he was put into an opaque box-like chamber which was then hermetically sealed. He was able to communicate with the doctors by means of a speaker but was forbidden to move one inch. Meanwhile, inside the box, the temperature was gently dropped down to near freezing point. When this was eventually achieved two cylindrical instruments slowly rotated across each other converging at a certain point into a ray which beamed precisely on to the affected part without, he said, causing any

167

pain. After a period the procedure was reversed and his body temperature was raised back to normal by a gentle 'de-frosting' process. It sounded like the most horrifying science fiction but he reassured me, telling me it was like a ballet and fascinating to watch although he admitted to a slight feeling of claustrophobia. Pressing me fervently to stay and have some more champagne, he went on talking right up to the time the nurses came to take him away.

As I left the hospital I marvelled again at his gallant spirit. His only show of fear—if indeed it could be called that—was his anxiety not to be left alone until the last moment. Never once had he complained against pain or the misfortune of his illness; in fact he jested he was grateful that he wouldn't have to put on that blasted black make-up for a long time!

At the weekend he convened more meetings with the *Three Sisters* production team and ran through certain scenes in the hospital room with some of the actors. He was getting more and more fractious due to his enforced confinement and his specialists came to the conclusion that, with his particular temperament, it would be beneficial to his recovery to allow him some freedom rather than try to restrain him. Consequently it was arranged for him to attend a run-through of the play for precisely two hours during a morning, before having one of his treatments. In utter secrecy he arrived in his own chauffeur-driven car, accompanied by one of the hospital doctors. Instantly he became totally involved in the rehearsal. The doctor, who had never seen actors working before, was fairly fascinated too. At the end of an hour-and-a-half he glanced at his watch to remind himself that his precious charge had to be returned on time. Five minutes before the time was up he whispered to Larry that they would have to leave; brushing this aside

Larry airily replied that he would do so when he was ready. Half-an-hour later, perspiring freely, the doctor insisted they must go. Probably to his surprise his hitherto meek and obedient patient turned to him and said pontifically, 'My dear sir, you and I are both professionals. I have been to *your* theatre, now you are in *mine* and I'm afraid I have not yet finished my job.' Chagrined, the gentleman withdrew in search of a telephone to explain why his parolee had mutinied. An hour later, a beaming Larry and a sheepish doctor left for the hospital. Heaven knows who's bottom Matron slapped.

However, Larry persuaded the authorities to allow him to be present at the final dress-rehearsals. The last treatment coincided with the first night of *Three Sisters* and, with a great show of bravura, he threatened to attend incognito. This, in fact, did not materialise, very wisely, because the immediate after-effects left him feeling weak and enervated. I promised to try and find out the critical reactions which my friends, the critics, were eager to give me at the conclusion of the play. I telephoned the hospital when I got home and was surprised—how silly can you get?—to hear lots of noisy laughter from his room! Joan had decided to take some champagne and a few friends from the cast to celebrate with him. He sounded very gay and cheerful and was delighted to hear my press news. Unobtrusively he attended a performance at the end of that week before 'allowing himself' to take a recuperative respite in Brighton.

I was spending the weekend at Chichester to be with David and answered a telephone in his office. It was a journalist politely enquiring for Larry's private Brighton number. I asked him if I could help and he told me he had just been informed that Vivien had died during the night. Personally shattered by the news I said I would ask Sir Laurence to call him. I rang Larry—who, of course, already knew—and commiserated with him. He was terribly upset and railed against the fates for their ill timing. She was starting rehearsals for a new play within a short while to which she was looking forward. He said he was going to London to offer any help to John Merivale, a great friend of Vivien's who shared the flat with her. Early the next morning the bell rang. It was answered by the housekeeper who was confronted by a man who claimed to be a personal friend of Miss Leigh. Believing this, in the circumstances, she let him in. He strolled into the flat, confronted Larry and Jack, admitted he was a journalist from the *Daily Express* and asked them for an exclusive. Wild with rage the two men turned on him and asked him to leave. He parried this threat with a plea to Larry for a 'little chat—man to man.' By now completely incensed they took him by the back of his jacket and frog marched him out of the flat. Vivien's funeral took place that week. One of the chief mourners was their life-long friend Cecil Tennant. Driving back from it to his house in the country the steering column suddenly broke causing him to lose control. The car hit a tree killing him instantaneously. This double tragedy, on top of Larry's own illness, was almost too much for my own moral courage, but I nerved myself to telephone yet again to offer my sympathies. As customary, when events become too great to take seriously, the reply was disarming. Having heard my condolences he said 'Do you know, my darling, I'm really no longer afraid of dying. I shan't be lonely; all my friends are up there.' A facile throwaway to cover his intense emotion.

While he had been absent from the theatre he had worried himself over the forced repertory changes in the Canadian tour and had come to the conclusion that, since he was unable to perform *Othello*, he should appear in all three of the plays as a slight recompense to the disappointed audiences. He asked to be included in the cast of the Feydeau farce, *A Flea In Her Ear*, in the relatively small role of Etienne, the butler. On the face of it, it sounded raving mad. To appear in all three plays, at every performance, for six weeks travelling from coast-to-coast of Canada, might be expected to tax the strength of someone who was perfectly fit: for a person recovering from a serious illness it seemed suicidal; but it was hopeless to try and dissuade him.

The official three-week holiday for the Company was scheduled at the end of July with resumption of rehearsals, both for Canada and the Old Vic, towards the end of August. Larry and Joan planned to go to Switzerland with the three children for part of the time. All the Company looked grey and shattered and desperately in need of a break. The administrative staff had to take their holidays as and when it was most convenient. In the circumstances it was impossible to go away at that juncture owing to the amount of preparation involved with the forthcoming tour. In Canada itself the National Theatre publicity was to be handled by two large commercial Public Relations firms but I had to deal with all press enquiries this end and all the information and material had to be correlated and sent by me from London.

At the end of the 'school hols' the sunburnt Company arrived back in the offices for rehearsals. The next new production to be performed at the Old Vic was the procrastinated all-male *As You Like It*. This had originally been announced for presentation in the spring to be directed by John Dexter and designed by Dacre Punt, with music by a pop singer. In the interim John had parted company with the National and the play had, of necessity, to be postponed. The new director was Clifford Williams, from the Royal Shakespeare Company, who had not previously worked for the National. By virtue of its apparently controversial casting *As You Like It*, when it was first announced, had provoked much titillative speculation and publicity. When the rehearsal date drew closer Larry asked me to do my best to pipe down on any publicity that might give the unusual casting a salacious slant, and not to allow any pictures to be taken during the rehearsals. The latter directive was an easy one because it had been one of the main concepts laid down in the general policy from the inception of the National. But some time earlier Ken Tynan and Clifford Williams had conversed together and had promised a Sunday newspaper an exclusive picture and rehearsal story; unfortunately nobody had informed me. When I discovered it, from a secretary, I went to Larry. I told him it would be comparatively simple for me to speak to the journalist and invoke our four-year-old edict of 'I'm terribly sorry but *nobody* is allowed into rehearsals' and assured him that I would take full blame for negating the promise. Ken was called to join us. When told my suggestion he said we would upset the journalist—who had been antagonistic toward the National in the past—and be foregoing valuable publicity. I tried to explain that, although he might be annoyed, he couldn't really damage us in print; any more than letting him have the exclusive would guarantee him being 'a good boy' in the future. I deferred to Larry who agreed with me; and asked if I could extricate us from the agreement without specifically involving his name or the National Theatre. I answered that was almost impossible. To me the irony of this predicament was heightened almost one year later on November 30th, 1968 in the *Daily Telegraph*. 'On December 19th the

172

National Theatre will open a new production of Shakespeare's *Love's Labour's Lost*, directed by Sir Laurence Olivier, who does not wish to discuss it before the opening. Nor does he want any of his cast to discuss it. Even the designer has been put out of bounds . . .' Larry enquired how well I knew Clifford Williams. I said I'd met him a number of times but didn't know him intimately. He, with Ken's knowledge, told me to have a word with Clifford and try to persuade him to talk to the journalist, saying that he had had second thoughts and changed his mind. I asked Clifford into my office and explained the problem. He was sympathetic and said he wouldn't have agreed if he had known about our 'house rules' because Stratford worked differently. However he, very understandably, said he had given his word to a journalist in good faith; did not wish to be embroiled in a policy issue; nor want an important feature writer prejudiced against him. Frankly, why should he? Ken joined us and told Clifford that Larry had an abhorrence toward press photographs tantamount to a 'persecution mania'. But the blasted ball was back in my court; I was on the horns of a dilemma and every other damned cliché in the book. Larry, not wishing the National—synonymous with his name—to be invoked; Clifford Williams anxious to 'go with' the policy but adamant about personal involvement; and I myself endeavouring to maintain my reputation for integrity with the press. Thinking in the frame-work of the non-exclusivity policy I tried to solve the problem. I reasoned that the solution would be to engage, as was customary, our own photographer (in this case Zoë Dominic) to take masses of pictures of rehearsals, fittings and the production. Thus having sufficient different shots to be distributed to various newspapers which would nullify the effect of an 'exclusive' in one paper. I outlined this plan to Larry who told me to go ahead. With due deference to him he had never understood how press representation worked; there's no reason why he should. When talking about it he once told me I was 'just a *head* shorter than Ken Tynan.' I took this to mean that he imagined Ken and I—in some strange transmogrification—did the same job. I had asked Ken if this was correct; his reply was 'Larry must be mad! I wouldn't even know where to start.' This hadn't stopped him plunging in impetuously from time to time.

Larry, rehearsing for Canada, was looking a tired man. Before leaving the hospital he had been warned he would experience certain specific after-effects from the treatment which would last for some months. They would cause him to suffer from deep depression accompanied by lack of concentration and momentary amnesia. Knowing he was still convalescent, everyone determined to cause him as little additional strain as possible. *The Dance of Death* opened the season and it was apparent that the illness had in no way impaired his acting; he was in terrific form. The first few weeks the company going to Canada played-in the three productions to prepare themselves for the tour. During this time I endeavoured to treat the *As You Like It* publicity with strict impartiality: although no writer—apart from the promised one—entered the rehearsals, I arranged various personal interviews with members of the cast and allotted different photographs. I had sent one of the morning nationals a picture which they were considering for publication. David, my husband, who was handling Chichester, had had a serious accident and was in hospital where I visited him at weekends. I went into his office and telephoned my secretary who sounded fraught. He told me that Ken, the previous evening, had heard about the photograph and had gone to Larry's office. I understood that he had persuaded

Larry to telephone the paper and personally ask them to stop publication of the picture. In return he had promised to give them an 'exclusive' interview when he came back from Canada. Horrified by this news I rang Larry in Brighton for confirmation. To my amazement he blamed me. He roared his head off at me and it took all my control not to say 'If you had backed me up sufficiently in the first place this would never have happened.' I didn't: I remembered he was still sick; took all his rage and offered him my apologies. I suffered my own rage afterwards for him and the invidious position he had placed himself in. I was hurt and ashamed for him.

The following week, the last before they left, I saw him frequently: neither of us referred to our telephone conversation. At one point he told me that, on his doctor's advice and with permission from the Board, Joan was flying over to Canada for a few days in the middle of the tour. This would necessitate her being absent for a couple of performances at the Vic. He asked if I thought I could keep it out of the press; mainly because he didn't want the public to think he was using his position for his own advantage. He was so perturbed over this aspect of a private issue that he called a general Company meeting and told them of his decision, explaining that he realised they would all miss their families but he knew he couldn't combat his depression without Joan; and begged their forgiveness. Unhesitatingly I promised to do my utmost to withhold it.

At the weekend I went to the airport with the usual television and press. They were departing from an unfamiliar building; time was drawing close to the take-off; there was no sign of Larry and the press were getting restless. One pompous little squirt said 'It'll leave any minute now—*without* the great Sir Laurence.' I replied that they'd look pretty silly in Canada if it arrived without him on board. Even though I knew it was a specially chartered flight, I was slightly anxious about him. But, some minutes before the scheduled departure, puffing and panting, he arrived. For the first time in years he had missed his train from Brighton to London. We pulled his leg, asking him why he hadn't hired a car from Brighton direct to the airport. He answered that, having missed the train, his only anxiety was getting to London, quite forgetting his destination was Canada! He was in a splendid mood: he joked with the press and gave the interviews. I went out with him to the plane. He kissed me before he boarded it and said 'Ginny darling, I'll never forgive you for that Friday night. Don't ever do it again.' Laughing, I promised I wouldn't and waved him goodbye.

As You Like It and the first performance of the tour co-incided on the same night, although, due to the time lag, the National curtain came down before the Canadian one went up. We had received an ovation with *As You* and telephoned them to say 'It's over and we're all right, Jack—now jolly good luck to you.'

I went on holiday for a couple of weeks and returned before the end of the Canadian tour. My reception in the offices seemed coolly remote: almost as if they were waiting for the teacher's verdict before deciding what attitude to adopt toward his 'pet'. It was spooky and unsettling; I blamed my imagination and tried to dismiss it. The company returned at the beginning of November. I met them and was delighted that Larry looked infinitely better than when I'd last seen him—in spite of the gruelling tour. He greeted me affectionately, as usual, and said how thrilled he was to be home. He rested for a few days, then submerged himself in administrative work; catching up with events during his absence and planning the repertoire for the spring.

The production in rehearsal was Molière's *Tartuffe*. This marked the first appearance of John Gielgud with the Company and Tyrone Guthrie's first production for the National; also the first French classical play to be presented by it. The reviews were not very enthusiastic; although, unanimously, the critics gave particular praise to Joan Plowright as Dorine, the pert French maid, a relatively small role. Naturally Larry was disappointed with the notices but pleased for Joan's sake.

Rehearsals for *Volpone*, the next production, started the following week—also directed by Tyrone Guthrie—due to open mid-January. The subsequent play was *Oedipus*, to be directed by Peter Brook. He had stipulated that he would require three months to stage it, and caused no little anxiety because he was living in Paris at that time; was engaged on other activities and extremely elusive to contact to settle the exact dates. This minor crisis occupied many agitated days with dozens of letters, cables and unproductive telephone calls but, like all the previous crises, resolved itself ultimately having taken a merry toll of wasted energy and jangled nerves.

One afternoon, just before Christmas, Larry strolled unheralded into my office, which he did frequently, and sat down for a chat. His opening question seemed an odd one: 'Did you see the Maharanee?' Taken by surprise I puzzled to think of a play with that title. I couldn't, so asked him who he meant. He said, 'You know, the one you were going to see some time ago.' It's uncanny how, without any forewarning, one gets a terrifying flash of insight into someone's mind, even more if you love and are close to them. In that split second, although I realised where he was leading, I

177

prayed he wouldn't press on with it. I became icy calm and cool as a computer and answered that she was a *Princess* not a Maharanee, adding I *had* seen her, nearly a year ago, and nothing had come of it. There was an ominous silence before poor Larry spoke again. With obvious distaste for his Sisyphean labour he proceeded to suggest to me that I should offer my resignation. This I declined to do. I reminded him of our agreement to a three-month trial: if I proved incapable of carrying out the job, or the job proved too much for my health we would terminate our association. I recalled the shows I'd publicised since I'd been back, and the difficult weeks spent coping with *Soldiers* in unusual circumstances. I asked him why he had not told me earlier that he was dissatisfied with me. He didn't give a clear answer. I remembered that during the probationary period he must have been too worried and alarmed about his illness (which would have showed some symptoms long before it was diagnosed) to have spared much thought to our bargain. I inwardly forgave him and pitied him his present task. Again he begged me to resign, saying it would be better for me. I couldn't see why and firmly refused; adding that I presumed I'd left him no option but to sack me. 'I'm afraid, my darling, as I can't persuade you to change your mind, that's about it.' I asked him to give me a reason. He reminded me of the muddle over *As You Like It* and the famous Black Friday night. He told me that one of his best friends was dying and had asked to see him that evening. Because of the press wrangle he had arrived too late. I hadn't known this and told him I was deeply sorry. I humbly suggested that it was the first time anything serious had gone wrong in my department and the punishment seemed a little harsh for one error in judgment; and couldn't be sufficient reason for dismissal. Reluctantly he replied it was a Board decision and 'a clash of personalities'.

178

Could be; could very easily be; but most certainly not with Larry himself. There was no more to be said.

Within minutes of his departure George Rowbottom, the general manager, appeared in my office with a form he said I had to sign but before doing so he wanted to make sure I fully understood it. With tears now coursing down my face I told him I didn't understand anything; much less a blasted form. However, I duly signed it. He then took me over to the local pub and bought me a few drinks. Later that night, a little tight, very stunned but determined to know the full reason for my dismissal, I telephoned Brighton. Joan answered the 'phone saying Larry wasn't available. I told her how upset I was and she said that he was, too. I begged her to give me some explanation. She reiterated that it was a Board decision and, in her own characteristic tones, vouchsafed a curious statement that Larry couldn't employ someone 'having the menopause'. This incorrectly hazarded conclusion convinced me there was no point in further discussion. Though, as I went to sleep, it didn't stop my mind boggling over the future of some actresses and female employees of uncertain age at the National! I asked George how many of the admin. staff, other than himself, knew of the situation. He replied no one except Kenneth Rae, the secretary to the Board. I'm afraid he was optimistic in this. Larry's glorious voice had been heard along the corridor, in the other offices, and news travels fast.

I had agreed to stay until after the opening of *Volpone*; but the following days spent in the office changed my mind. Isolated, with a touch of leprosy, I decided I was not doing any further good to the National and went to Larry's sound-proofed office for a final talk. He was kind and affectionate as always and offered to give me any 'dossier' (his own odd word in the circumstances!) I might need, which I declined with many thanks. On Saturday morning, with the offices empty, I went to collect my personal belongings. There were no false speeches of regret, thank God! No inscribed silver memento; no letters of gratitude for National service rendered! I mused on the past twenty years of knowing Larry: this remarkable, complex man whom I believe to be an example of that indiscriminately used word 'genius', which he would deny violently—and possibly use violence to me for daring to apply it to him. At the beginning I didn't believe, illogically, the end would ever come. But as I walked along the corridor of inadequate offices for the last time I realised sadly there wasn't room for loyalty and power.

INDEX